Big Land, Big Sky, Big Hair:
Best of the Texas Poetry Calendar

BIGLand, BIGSky, BIGHair:

Best of the Texas Poetry Calendar

Scott Wiggerman, Editor
Jason Robberson, Assistant Editor

David Meischen, Managing Editor
Kristee Humphrey, Graphic Designer

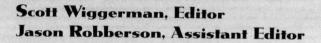 **DOS GATOS PRESS**

Austin, Texas

Big Land, Big Sky, Big Hair:
Best of the Texas Poetry Calendar
© 2008, Dos Gatos Press
ISBN-13: 978-09760051-4-8

Special thanks to Julia Hu, who proofread the entire manuscript, and to the many poets, especially Anthony Russell White and Lianne Elizabeth Mercer, who helped locate those who had "disappeared" over the course of a decade.

Dos Gatos Press
1310 Crestwood Rd.
Austin, TX 78722
www.dosgatospress.org

Dos Gatos Press is a non-profit, tax-exempt corporation organized for literary and educational purposes. Our goals are to make poetry more widely available to the reading public and to support writers of poetry—especially in Texas and the Southwest.

I. If Ghosts Could Speak: Texas People

II. What's Next in Eden: Texas Flora & Fauna

III. Between Here and the Horizon: Texas Places

IV. Logic of the Air: Texas Weather & Seasons

I. If Ghosts Could Speak: Texas People

Time Exposure

In the early spring of our lives
we had been sweethearts, but time
played loose with an out-of-season chill.
In the late autumn of our lives
we became lovers, and time
compensated with an out-of-season heat.

To avoid small-town eyes
we spent time at the ranch
where his courtly gifts
were released in private.
"I want to show you something.
We will go in the Jeep after supper."

Clear skies held to Texas myth.
Insects sang songs of night.
"Watch over there by that clump of oaks."
He aimed the spotlight, pressed a switch, and
instantly! a herd of deer—phantoms
of fantasia—leapt! into the air.

Just as quickly, their brief
burst of beauty disappeared.
I caught my breath, reached for his arm,
and began to understand why,
when I had left to see the world,
he had stayed to tend the land.

Mary-Agnes Taylor

Rising Star, Texas 1898/1992

I have not
perceived the why
of her bones' calling,
the slack decay
in quiet darkness,
unmeddled for nine decades,
but she does not let me rest.
Tubercular, birth-drained,
she slipped away
from the prairie,
the wagon, her husband's arms
into the wider Texas night,
ten stars flung back across her shoulder,
three small daughters
bundled off to Antelope
and Grandma Crossman's care.

R. W. rode north
toward Oklahoma's vastness,
sending money back
for a stone.
But we have searched and searched,
walked dusty paths from iron fence
to iron fence, read leaden plaques,
righted each crude wooden marker,
paused at each blanched stone to read,
and have not found a trace
of any resting-place
for grandma's mother.

No stone
in Rising Star
marks
Emma Valentine's
narrow sleep.

Carol Cullar

4

Opening Day

In Ellis County, dove weed grows up
along the road like a wall
hiding crimped maize stalks
and empty cotton fields.
Walking, gun bent open
to prove to my sons I practice what I preach,
I breathe in hard
times, memories of days I walked
this rutted stretch of rusty dust on my own
first hunt, my father's stride exacting
two of mine. Boys, I say,
in a voice they recognize
as a story start,
when I was not much younger
than you two are now,
your grandfather taught me
about hunting: how to tell the difference
between a killdee and a dove,
how to spot a line of birds coming hard
and fast up a creek bed, how to drop below
the Johnson grass and lead the line,
taking the second bird
with my first shot,
how to follow its fall into the orchard,
how to find the bird,
step on its body
and snatch off the head
before I could think twice
about the beauty
of its breath beneath
silver-gray feathers and fluttering wings
which beat hard and fast,
high above boys
on the road to manhood.

Anne McCrady

Pioneer Grave

The light of her young life went down,
As sinks behind the hill,
The glory of a setting star,
Clear suddenly, and still.
         Epitaph, Hattie Haby
         January 26, 1881–January 2, 1897

Jack and Hattie arrived in Texas, homesteading in their hearts,
their baby in her womb. They settled near a creek embraced
by limestone canyons—one of the highest reaches
in the state's Hill Country, a stretch now called The Divide.

Jack and Hattie framed dreams in a one-room cabin,
planted hope in a pear orchard nurtured by artesian springs
in rocky soil. Buffalo grass wove blankets across the hills,
deer ran trails along their creek.

Jack said good-bye to Hattie beside that very creek,
buried their baby at her breast, no name to mark its birth,
still, and cold, like that first winter.

                              Anne Schneider

Ceniza / Ash

Like six monks unable to sleep
in the darkness of a mountain
hamlet, my friends and I sit
on a porch in north Dallas
and grind the hours away like
stubbing out the dregs of the
Cuban cigars we shared; there
in the beetle-black fingers of night,
our fugitive corollas blazed, each
of us working to scorch away the
black wings that shuddered through

the air, our separation looming
*como los relámpagos negros sobre
las cordilleras.* I think of what it
would be like to be gone for good,
not moving beneath the uncharmed
stars, but death, gone-ness, the black
and sugarless void that no great
gospel song praises, the Christ-ether
of blank. I re-light my fading cigar,
tap new ash into the gray ceramic
bowl, wanting to say *Pray for me, pray
for us all*, but I swallow those words,
their bitter nourishment, and like a
restless spirit, I became lost once more
in longing, the half-lit bliss of reverie
among friends who, speechless, share most.

Ryan G. Van Cleave

The Pol

I'm a polite little person with a brave little smile
And go about business with nary a wile.
My manners are perfect: you've seen me at dinner.
I eat with the silver from outer to inner.
I stand when the elderly enter the door
and listen enchanted to seniors who bore.
I was elected to office with the refrain
of leading the poor up the ladder again.
I thank for all favors with elegant notes,
withstanding temptation of soliciting votes.
I've spiked up the budget from recent malaise
(increasing my income in various ways).
When the good Lord has called me, I'll lie in repose
in a white silken gown from my toes to my nose.
I'll go straight to heaven where I'll gladly inscribe
your name in the Book in return for a bribe.

Katie O'Sullivan

At the Sweetheart Dances

(when my Daddy taught me how)

I bumped the tips of his black dress shoes,
kicked my foot into his shin, but he never, never
stopped dancing or said, "Ouch," just kept me moving
to the *cumbia* beat of bass and saxophone as he held me
and danced us along the floor, in to me and out
from me while we followed the other Men's Club members
dancing with their wives or daughters in the *cumbia*
circle until Paul Elizondo's orchestra would slide
into a romantic *ranchera* and Daddy would press his arm
around my waist and weave us through couples,
suddenly swaying as he crooned the Spanish lyrics in my
ear, only to thrust me away, twirl me under his arm with
only my gasp and his fingertips keeping us together until
he caught me again, kept me on my feet, and before I
could catch my breath, we moved on to a lively melody,
our shoulders pumping away as he told me to holler a *grito*
while he bounced our *polkas* over the dance floor.

DIANE GONZALES BERTRAND

Cowboy

I ride
under the carapace
of sky,
sigh ballads
with the wind.
My steed's feet
stir up dust devils
of sandy earth,
dried sage,
rootless tumbleweed.

SHERYL SLOCUM

THE PRAYERS OF DOLORES PEREZ

Dolores Perez prayed,
on knees as swollen as grapefruit.
She prayed for her neighbor Astacio,
the Sears service man with lung cancer.
Astacio had fixed her TV and washing machine.
She paid him with constant prayers.
Dolores prayed as she patted tortillas.
She prayed for her dead husband and daughter.
She prayed each step to the bus stop.
At Mass, she knelt beside Anna,
who asked God to heal her unborn baby,
malformed, the doctor had told her.
Dolores laid her hand on Anna's belly and prayed.
Each night on her porch,
Dolores listened for the voice of God.
She heard only wind,
rustling the leaves of the sycamore tree.
She watched for angels,
looking closely at white moths,
fluttering against the screen door.
She hoped for dreams of the Virgin,
but arthritis made her sleep fitful.
Waking, she remembered no visions.
Dolores Perez died.
Her granddaughter gave the TV and washer to Goodwill,
and put a For Sale sign in the yard.
Astacio, back on service calls,
missed his neighbor, his cancer cured.
Anna's baby was born perfect.
"I can't explain it," the doctor said.
Outside Dolores' empty house,
wind rustled the leaves in the sycamore tree,
white moths fluttered against the screen door.

SHELLIE LYON

Blind Lemon Jefferson's Body Is Brought from Chicago to Wortham, Texas, by Pianist and Labelmate Will Ezell

New Year's Day, 1930

No car, no chauffeur. Two ashen horses
nicker wet and close through the storm's static,
each hoof strikes a nail in the coffin's lid.
It's not the blizzard's ardor stayed church bells:
it's the weight of unmoored boys underground.
Stayed, the heart—in fields opening wide between beats—
sinks below the rhythmic counterpoints
of abundant drought and scant harvest.
Stayed, the mind—under the years' chorded streams—
revisits bright, bright green seedlings strumming
in warming furrows, the feracious Texas soil
turning itself inside out, steaming, to receive.

JUDY JENSEN

Angelina

Tourists fly to Austin to see a capitol building
taller than the one in Washington.
On daily drives up Congress Avenue,
I hardly notice that monument. Like tourists though
I pass your statue, matron Angelina Eberly,
and each time you ignite in me
a chuckle, a pride in Austin's weirdness,
and a spiteful smirk toward that fly-trap
on the bayou. Twice-widowed Angelina,
on December 29, 1842, you fired a cannon,
defaced the Land Grant Building,
and woke a sleeping Austin to Houston's
ego-driven documental abduction.
Even after your warning shot, the thieves
hauled state papers eighteen miles
toward Houston before Austin vigilantes,

an ad hoc Committee of Safety, caught up,
reversed the robbery, and rolled those wagons
back to Central Texas where they belong.
I expect your erstwhile tenant, Sam Houston,
never stayed with you again,
but when a Sixth Street red light stops me,
I smile at the Capitol and nod respectfully
toward you, Mrs. Angelina Eberly.
When we recall your bloodless Archives War
you wake us up again.

Robert Elzy Cogswell

How They Ate in El Paso, 1932

A man climbed up onto the roof of a little stucco diner.
He carried a sack, one of those canvas sacks
for bank deposits—but no one
deposited money in a bank anymore.
This sack was filled with pennies and nickels,
which the man began to toss to the street below,
scattering handfuls while a crowd gathered,
people rushing from across the street, pouring out
from hotels and seedy tourist camp courts.

Then the man invited them all to come into his diner.
He climbed down from his roof.
He put on his apron and cooked hamburgers on his grill.
Anyone who'd found a nickel could buy a five-cent burger,
or a five-cent piece of pie, peach or cherry,
buttermilk, banana cream—they would have to choose.

The man's diner was filled with strangers sharing tables,
festive, as if about to break into song or dance in the aisles
while the scent of frying meat filled the air.
Not one of these people would ask the man if he was crazy.
No one would tell him, *This is no way to run a business.*

Karen Peterson

My Next Fifty

I'll live grandly
my next fifty years:
take out a second mortgage,
get a gold Visa,
travel to Pago Pago,
lie naked in the sun
with bronze-colored natives,
sip rum from a pineapple,
watch sweat trickle down
hard muscles.
And when the children ask
where I have been,
I'll lie and say,
"A senior citizen tour
to visit the Pope."

I'll cash in the life insurance,
buy diamonds and chiffon dresses
with plunging necklines
I'll wear to Safeway,
eat giant shrimp by the pound
and the freshest pastries,
find my Gloria Swanson cigarette holder
and start smoking again,
use my best crystal to drink
the finest brandy and champagne
until the sun rises.
And when the children ask
about their inheritance,
I'll lie and say, "Not to worry,
it's been taken care of."

Lana Book

Let Me Love You in Texan

after Laure-Anne Bosselaar's "Let Me Love You in Flemish"

Let me love you in Texan tonight—words
flashy as red pickups and low-slung ranchettes,
wrought-iron gates corralling their peacocks.

I know words slinky as bayous
in concrete canals snaking through tropical suburbs
to barges and shrimpers in sulphur ship channels.

Glinty windows of skyscrapers or
Gulf's cumulus spectacle. Tex-Mex
sassy as two-step or
rodeo riders on Astrodome trails.

Taste my tongue, sizzly jalapeño
on flour-tortilla "white death."
The tequila is lethal, cerveza's
cool bubbles tingle guacamole and chips.

I don't know the *habla* of *Español*,
of the soft brown-eyed women, their
bougainvillea abundant and silent,

but let me love you with syllables over-
heard here, words the shy-tongued
construction workers murmur in salsa:

Ese lunar que tienes,
cielito lindo, junto a la boca,
no se lo des a nadie
cielito lindo, que a mí me toca.

SALLY WELLS RIDGWAY

Witness to Nine-One-One

There are things you don't plan that just happen. One Saturday night, almost after dinner, my husband put down his spoon and tipped sideways out of his chair. I caught him, holding until he opened his eyes. Then I could pick up the phone, punch three magic numbers, and steady my voice. A siren and six minutes later, our dining room filled with tall young men, knowing exactly what to do. When he was stabilized and talking,

they trundled him out the door. I looked at the dinner table. "Leave it," said the last young man. I put my husband's ice cream in the freezer and left lights burning. The urgent howl of the ambulance parted traffic like a comb all the way to the Houston Medical Center, tall buildings of healing, always bright-lit. Delivered, the patient was prodded, listened to, charted. A tree of hospital hardware sprouted by his bed.

Later, the team that had brought us in, stopped after another run, stood around his bed and beamed. Thankful for skills and attentions, he rested, ready to stay. Three a.m., I went home to the deserted dinner table, washed the empty dishes in the empty kitchen, cleaned counters, and prayed for us all. Then for comfort—although more was in a carton—I got out my husband's dish of ice cream and finished it up.

Jean H. Marvin

In My Father's Shop

I would hear him before I saw him—
I would hear some strange German hymn
blending with the hum of the whirring bellows.

He would nod a welcome,
his bald pate reflecting pink,
and with clenched tongs
take from the forge
a strip of purple-hot metal
that seemed to pulse as if alive.

On the heel of the anvil
his ball-peen hammer
did a little tap dance of pings—
a foreplay of the calculated blows
that on the anvil's horn
shape-shifted the ribbon of iron
into curls and angles
that defined the sacred signs
of Texas cattle brands: the lazy S, the rocking R.

When a brand was finished
he would burn it into one
of the large double doors
that had over time become
giant tablets of Western hieroglyphics.

A sense of burning pine lingers
as does a pity for burning hide.

MARY-AGNES TAYLOR

Ventanas Llorando

The once-white stucco building stands tall
and deserted, windows covered with rotting plywood.

A baby girl was born there in 1960;
later her brother lay on the ER table,
one foot pointing the wrong direction,
like Jem's arm, from a horse fall;
then her white-haired grandfather lifeless,
cancer victorious.

Now she drives by on her way somewhere else
pretending not to listen to
what boarded windows weep.

MARY MARGARET DOUGHERTY

Joe's Barbeque

If it's something he loves—
say, a parking-lot party
after the hordes have peeled away
in search of other noise—
when everything still left
is what he loves most anyway—
Chet Baker on the boom box,
an armful of sleepy woman—
when you stick around, you'll find
that every last unforgettable morsel
is as smoky
and tender
and sweet
and slow
as the slabs of good cow
being saved for tomorrow's sandwiches.

Peggy Lin Duthie

High Plains Homesteader

He was gaunt as a fence post, burdened to bleakness;
his hands were great vises for clamping work—controlling
bucking plowshares, stubborn mules and stumps, clearing the way

for corn and cotton and a little cash. No shirt sleeve
was long enough; his big-boned wrists, gnarly as oak root,
hinged his best and most-used tools—those powerful hands.

Black-hatted and roughshod, he trod the fields, high-tops
caked in spring mud and the cow lot, a High Plains settler.
But he was more than that—he was a Panhandle giant

who clawed and combed the earth, seeded it to his family's needs,
gathered the yield by muscle and sweat and a tireless will
that could bear the blistering sun and wind and blowing dirt.

His eyes were gatherers, too—of the distant spaces—
surveying the wide plains of promise, the reaching sky,
the future. They were sky-colored, infinity blue;

their hawk-like glare could stare down any bold challenge
or threat. They looked at a clearing and saw growing grain,
at empty stretches across the Caprock and saw herds . . .

and towns, stores, schools, churches. They saw a seeded future
springing up. Under the shade of that big black hat brim,
the clear eyes of the plainsman held the light of endless hope.

James O. Dobbs

I Am Lucy

I am the old, wrinkled, pipe-smoking woman
living in a dingy efficiency of a cheap hotel.

When I die, the world will think this is all of me,
unless I tell them I laid lovingly on the
breast of a mama. They will not know I rescued
broken birds and soothed sisters once I had left
the mother I called Alice to move like a tadpole in
the water of humanity, waiting for my legs.

I should tell them I danced the polka
and sang in my heart with John Phillips,
a man fashioned from pig iron and pudding.
Married him I did, bore six children with our
melded souls. All six gone now to pass us on,
give us our place in other souls, other lives.

Unless I tell them, they will never know I am a
thousand years of joy and tears, that each line in
my leathery face is a gift I gave.

Betty Davis

Targets

Each fall the hunters migrate to my town
in annual pursuit of trophy deer.
They come with guns and tents and money, down-
filled sleeping bags, loud curses and cold beer.
And every single season drivers stop
their buck-draped cars beside me and request
directions to King's Taxidermy Shop.
I tell them at the granite house head west
to Lou's Fine Diner, then go south a way.
I could have said the stone home's where Gus Doone
still lives. His wife just died. And Lisa Kay,
Lou's oldest daughter, will be getting married soon.
I could have said all that, exactly word
for word. But hunters, they would not have heard.

Aliene Pylant

Free Concert in the Park

Dragging a scavenged waterbed bag
a man gathers cans
in the park, blanket by blanket
picnickers make their donations.
One drunk guy gives
a hook-shot can-toss
right into the bag
— 2 points! —
and his girlfriend laughs.
The can man moves on,
turns away from the moment,
but I'm still in it,
I'm still on the arc of the can.
I get lost at these intersections,
someone please spin me & point me away—
past cartwheeling kids with running lights on their shoes,
past Crazy Carl

doing a snaky dance
to imaginary trombone music,
toward the bats flowing out with nightfall
like a river of quarter-notes,
syncopated,
the jazz of another world.

SUZANNE FREEMAN

CLEANING GRAVES IN CALVERT

for papa johnny hodge, my great-great grandfather

under a crying elder willow
we met. the 107 degree shade
bearing thirsty earth
from which i sprang.

a safehouse next door to
a tinderbox church.
sanctuary from hot

lone star nights.
though your face is hidden
i feel you
in the folds of mama's hands.

in my blood
i hear you. calling
beyond tired summer
crops to bring us here.

ritual precedes emancipation
(we were the last to know).
scrubbing dirt from your headstone.
gathering scattered branches.

QURAYSH ALI LANSANA

Wild Bill Bailey

Wild Bill Bailey, so the neighbors all say,
stands tall in his grave waiting Judgment Day
on Bailey's Prairie, where his lantern light
flits blue through the trees on a moonless night.
Wild roses ramble high above his head.
They say he wanders, that unruly dead,
perhaps for a drink, if the jug's gone dry
that they laid at his feet, those years gone by.
Let him pass, his light and his gun in hand;
He was Houston's friend, and a fearless man.

Geneva Fulgham

February

It arrives each February: a red envelope containing two foil-wrapped chocolate hearts and bearing no return address, having followed her across eighteen years, six states, eight homes, three careers.

She wonders how the sender always finds her, each message composed of words sliced from newspapers, a ransom note holding someone's heart hostage, its anonymous text unvarying:

You Were Born to be Mine, Why Even Fight It.

Not a question, a statement.

She's not sure whether to feel flattered or threatened. Perhaps it's a prank by her brother to whom she once confided that life seemed devoid of romantic possibilities ever since she'd left Texas.

But February passes with no red envelope, no chocolates. She feels relief, mostly—yes, relief!—but tinged with something like regret, something like curiosity, wondering whether the author merely gave up or died, leaving behind a mystery that will never be solved.

Erica Lehrer

Breakfast at Denny's in Pasadena

I'm at Denny's and I've just ordered
the Senior French Slam, my maiden Slam:
I'm now 55 and legal.

But in this hot-flash-hot room,
I'm the bride, the kindergartner on her first day of school.
My fellow diners think I'm young
on my first day of being old at Denny's.
Old guys ogle me,
and the older old women—the ones
who've stopped considering face-lifts—
glance sideways at my less droopy turkey wattles,
my just-dyed hair with its perky perm
and my last-all-day lipstick and dieting hips.
I am driven to push my Slam aside and clamber
up onto my table and shout:
Good morning!
I'm announcing today to you all
that I'm still keeping up this lawn, by God!
I'll never let moss grow on me, or weeds,
like that gray woman plunging into pancakes at table 3.
When I have my fatal coronary,
I want to stumble over in high-heeled boots.
As I sink to the floor, I'll regret dirtying
my red velvet jeans, dry-clean-only.

So don't just sit there and stare, mouths
agape, syrupy forks poised in mid-air.
Rather, raise your coffee cups in a toast, for
I do solemnly swear this morning at Denny's in Pasadena:
I shall not go gentle or unmade-up into that good night.

Mary G. Parham

21

Produce Corner

After a grocery cart chat
with a casual acquaintance
about the sweetness of apples,
tender green asparagus,
the high cost of tomatoes,
the scarcity of figs,
she leans into me and
quietly announces,
"I'm going to get a cat.
I miss being touched."
And I begin to understand
the sadness in her smile.

Ann Reisfeld Boutté

They Follow Dreams

They follow dreams of money, cars and clothes
from squalid towns where chickens soil the street.
The stream of seekers, never-ending, flows
along a trail through arid scrub mesquite.

The smuggler hawks the hope for work, the meat
illegals hunger for, but hides the woes
that challenge wills enduring devil's heat.
They follow dreams of money, cars and clothes.

Across the Rio Grande, the future glows.
They gamble for a taste of labor's sweet
reward. The smuggler holds the deck; he knows
the squalid towns where chickens soil the street.

High spirits match the morning's steady beat,
but midday sun weighs heavy, cadence slows
past bones recalling yesteryear's defeat.
The stream of seekers, never-ending, flows

past sandy mounds. Stick crosses speak of those
who lagged behind, of those who chose retreat,
who heard the bird of ill emit three crows
along the trail through arid scrub mesquite.

Though desert blisters tender yearning feet,
the paths to gainful jobs in cities pose
a better life. With scant to drink or eat
through cruel land, the deadly tally grows.
They follow dreams.

VIRGINIA FREY

A NEW WORLD

Dallas, circa 1957

We sit around Grandmother's Sunday table
for lunch which, country-born, she calls dinner,
holding memories of men coming in from the fields,
unlike this city life and her modest home
where the railroad tracks across the street still run
through her mind to an older world almost disappeared.

I survey the beaded iced tea glasses
the bowls of steaming vegetables and fried chicken,
and absorb talk of the day's wonders: the mystical
electric door-opener at the grocery store,
the missing neighborhood just beyond the tracks
cleared for a runway to hold the new jet traffic.

Sometimes the trains and jets join forces to halt
the conversation, suspending our words in midair,
hostage to the all-embracing sound
while we wait with optimistic smiles,
the silver and china rattling, our table a foreign
vessel hurling us into our brilliant future.

JOHN G. HAMMOND

The Preacher's Wife

She was loud as a bluejay
harassing a cat,
persistent as a dog barking
in the next yard.
Four inches taller
than her husband, she always

wore high heels, owned
every room she walked into,
church members afraid she'd drop
what was whispered to her husband.
The minister, so kind and patient—
only his sermons uninterrupted—

died suddenly one Tuesday morning.
She took to her bed, seemed
to hear other voices.
Well, only God knows the balance
in any marriage. Five days later,
following her leader, she died.

Jean H. Marvin

Texas Two-Step

He invited.
She accepted.
He enjoyed.
She endured.
He cajoled.
She refused.
He sent wildflowers.
She smiled vaguely.
He wrote notes.
She didn't answer.
He came by.
She hid out.

Life moved on.
While waiting in
The check-out line
She saw his face
On the cover of *Time*.

Kay Gorges Schill

Legacies

Just this side of El Paso, the names
of towns roll over the tongue like
the sweet, smooth taste of flan:
Sierra Blanca, Esperanza,
Alamo Alto, and Acala—
legacies left by the conquistadors
in their elusive quest
for glory and for gold.

But McNary jars the senses
like finding a potato
growing among the papayas,
and the questions of how and why
roll across the desert
like restless tumbleweeds.

Two thousand miles away
and four generations ago,
Grandmother had an uncle,
the black sheep with
pearl-handled pistols
and a thirst for adventure.

If ghosts could speak,
what could memory tell
about this tired place sleeping
under the blue morning sun?

Sheila Tingley Moore

Two Characters, One Plot

We are exactly unalike. She is taller,
more substantial bone for bone. Her presence
fills a room, voice booms & laughter rumbles:
frequent thunder in summer storm.
She is streaming waist-length hair,
chicken-fried steak, marching bands—to my
tussled curl, windchimes, cream cheese & olive.
Her: blood-red, ruby-red, beet-red—a force
to be reckoned with. Me? Passive resistance,
periwinkle. She's left. I'm right.
I am Dallas. She is Ft. Worth.

What binds us is books. She knows
author, publishing house, minuscule detail
of every plot, each obscure character.
I know what I like. We seek out-of-the-way
second-hand bookshops around Ft. Worth,
Dallas and beyond. Expect
some obscure first edition to tumble
into our hands.

She drives; I buy lunch. Together
we eat our way through every restaurant,
luncheonette & greasy spoon
in Margaret Moseley's current series.
When we die, we'll go to Archer City.

Ann Howells

Martha's Liberation

Like other muted women
of her generation
Aunt Martha was tunnel-trained
in matters of duty to family
and duty to God.

In unerring repetition
she moved through domestic pantomimes
set in scripted weeks
that began with wash pots
and ended in a pew.

When her body was found
near the chicken coop
caught on a barbed wire fence
with Uncle Charlie's gun nearby,
neat rows of Saturday's pies
were still cooling in the kitchen.

Father de Castro instructed
doubting church members
that Martha's wounds were indeed
accidental, and
upon extolling her exemplary life
so biblical in nature
he sanctioned a Christian burial
in sanctified soil.

MARY-AGNES TAYLOR

WILDCATTING

Down goes another length of dirty drillpipe.
Sullen crew, but Fridays they cash their paychecks.
Stinking drilling mud everywhere—and no promises.
Worthless prospect, say the critics,
their money goes where it has company.
A wacko dowser, they call me,
because I know this is the place.
I see a pipeline from this desolate spot,
a flowing source of wonder and riches.
Just a little more pipe.
We're almost there.
I can smell it.

ANTHONY RUSSELL WHITE

Texas Boy at Ten

At ten I was a Texas farm boy
Ready to join Odysseus,
Eager to meet my Cyclops,
Fearless of the Sirens' song.

I was up before dawn the day the new tractor came,
Begging my sunburned father to give me the reins.

He looked me over, silently taking my measure,
Drove the tractor down to a large fallow field
With me on the hitch, hardly hanging on.

I climbed into that massive seat
As my father set the engine speed,
Leaped off, leaving me alone
Like Phaeton in charge of the sun.

Hungry horses are hard to control,
I turned to Helios for help.
I see his sunny face even now,
Simply laughing and laughing

As I flew around the radiant world,
Savoring my first terrifying taste of power,
Master of the Dawn.

G. A. Hottel

Men with Guns and Pickups

Two Texans I know, handsome men, gun-racks
in their pickups, meet for the first time
over smells of grilled meat and spilled beer.

As a newcomer here from the northeast,
New Yorker stereotypes crowd my mind.
I fret as these two size each other up,

match virtues of jet ski against wave rider.
The divorced one proudly tells us
about his visiting three-year-old,

how the boy saw the clouds at sunset
come down like the wings of a hawk
the way Basho saw the crow-dark wings

of night settle on withered branches.
What gets me is that the other guy,
childless, gray-haired, had eyes full of sparklers.

Marilynn Talal

Sunrise, Galveston

From the deck, the first sliver of rising sun
and he's back on the Mississippi Gulf Coast,
a small boy who creeps from his hotel room
down to the kitchen of the Buena Vista
to collect crabnet, bait, and bucket,
then trudges across the highway, onto the pier.
He drops his net, looks up to see a slim red arc,
its bounce across waves, and he's amazed
that tiny slice of red could later blaze
into bright daylight.

Now, seventy years later, sleep-weary,
he's awake long before the rest of the house.
With his coffee, his mystery, he wanders
the deck and finds this memory,
long fallow. Today he's amazed
that in spite of ceaseless tragic news,
that brilliant, rosy curve in the east
will brighten, grow round and appear
to rise over the Gulf—his world still turning.

Trudy S. Guinee

Iron Works

My mother's father was a Llano blacksmith,
a steel percussionist whose hammer slapped
a beat which threatened to explode his shop

the day another daughter came along—the fifth.
No sons! His wounded German pride grew chapped
to think a legacy of metalwork would stop.

His artistry with iron was almost myth—
a man of steel who forged the brands and tapped
the shoes on skittish horses other blacksmiths dropped.

My mother's mother, who forgave his tizzy,
sang Brahms while laundering small dresses
with sashes, bows and ruffled pinafores.

Five daughters kept her Monday washdays busy,
scrubbing, bleaching, bluing all the messes.
Then Tuesday's ironing by the stove indoors,

with heated implements that made her dizzy—
crimping, pleating, fluting to perfection. Her finesse
with iron considered just another household chore.

Aliene Pylant

Seniors. Temple, Texas.

They stand inside a circle
of pickup trucks and SUVs,
gimme caps pointed at the ground
between them as they stir
the sandy dirt with their boot tips,
fingers slipped halfway into pockets,
elbows loose, shirt sleeves rolled,
no one the leader, no one less.

Spitting into the dust,
for old time's sake
they talk about girls
who never wear bras,
mothers who still make lunches
and the addictions of hardworking men
who raised them to leave all this
one day for college or work . . . or war.

Anne McCrady

Early in the Morning, on the Road, near Franklin, Texas

Her skirt clings to her the way fog clings to a flower.
Her legs are curled up, her sleeping face soft like a saint.
Driving for hours a man thinks about how things are measured,
about how coffee always tastes better in small towns.

Her legs are curled up, her sleeping face soft like a saint.
St. Augustine said the eye is attracted to beautiful objects.
Coffee always tastes better in small towns;
the treasures of the destination make us take the trip.

St. Augustine said the eye is attracted to beautiful objects.
The full moon makes her skin glow like a statue.
The treasures en route make us take the trip.
I start out thinking in terms of miles and hours

but the full moon makes her skin translucent like a statue.
Her breathing is as fragrant and sure as moonflowers
and I stop thinking in terms of miles and hours.
She'll wake up in a little while and touch me with her bare toe.

But for now, her breathing is as fragrant as moonflowers.
Driving for hours a man thinks about what makes things holy.
She'll wake up in a little while and bless me with her bare toe,
her skirt clinging to her the way fog caresses a flower.

Alan Birkelbach

Remember the Alamo: Texas-Born Mexican

Straddling a
History no one talks about,
We jump-rope a moving border,
Lasso our children with it
and fly our
Texas Flag
Everywhere we go
(spitting at the
New Englanders
who think it brash)

Yes, I love my state

and I love my
Brown hair, my
Brown blood, my
Brown man and the
Brown babies I raise
to remember the Alamo

Laurie A. Guerrero

Georgia O'Keeffe in Texas

When light comes to the plains
and the evening star rises I am alone,
loving the sky.
I find a door
in the square, I paint
my way into the world—
the bulging orb,
the undulating line, the flower
opening.

I want everything all at once,
to go where the windmills
jut from the plains, to ride

into Amarillo, hear
the loud saloons, the boots
on wooden sidewalks,

then slide into Palo Duro,
the quiet canyon, as into sleep—
a slit in the nothingness,
a waterfall. I want to walk
into that wide sunset space
with the stars.

In the end,
isn't it all memory,
the flower opening, the train
trailing smoke in the Texas night?

LEE ROBINSON

STELLA

Your voice hums East Texas,
storying, tall taling, true telling:
the skunk drowned in the lard can,
your grandmother forded rivers,
your father fiddled *Good Night Ladies*
to mark the end of star-lit socials.
All the while your hands birth
pies, another batch of biscuits,
steadily moving food to us.
Named for your father, Johnnie Estelle,
country you call it,
your daughter given one seemly name.
Praise gainsaid as blindness
to your ways—if I'd but
known you when. Now is good,
my mother-in-law, who came
late to my life and blessed it.

MEREDITH TREDE

Just Outside of Bobo, Texas

I used to be afraid of that old man, my friend's
grandfather. I'd spend the night on their farm
and watch him work all day. While we played
in the hay, he slopped pigs; while we fished
for bass in the man-made ponds, he drove
the tractor in the cornfields; while we hunted
for arrowheads in the freshly tilled soil, he severed
a chicken's head for dinner. He never looked up
from his labors. And after dinner he would sit
in his chair and watch the news, then go to bed
early. Until one night, while I was playing gin
rummy with my friend and sneaking stares at him
from across the room, he asked me, "Boy . . .
how old do you think I am?" Then he spit tobacco
into his spittoon. I didn't want to be cruel,
so I thought I'd guess low. I looked at his sinewy
neck, weathered face, as brown as the soil
he'd turned that day, his hunched back, his
gnarled hands—purple veins separating fingers
like a delta. His toothless smile, sparse gray
and white hair. "Eighty?" I ventured. He cackled,
"Boy, I'm 62 years old!" He spit again across the room,
winking his crystal-clear sky-blue eye.

BRADLEY EARLE HOGE

Nana's Apron

Made from bleached-white flour sacks and decorated with designs
embroidered by light of a kerosene lamp, its once-brilliant colors faded
from lye soap washings and drying in hot Texas sun.

When held by the hem, it was large enough to carry tomatoes and beans
picked from the garden, roses for the table, feathers for pillows from a
fresh-plucked chicken.

Wrapped around me like a cocoon, her apron protected my clothes from childhood mishaps as she taught me to cook and bake. A large pocket often hid a stick of gum or an all-day sucker, most times discovered with dough-covered hands.

Now it hangs in my own kitchen, reminding me daily of homemade bread, dewberry jelly, home-churned butter, and love.

CAROL J. RHODES

Honk If You're My Daddy

The thing is—
I couldn't be sure,
being that you never waved or nothin'

But I remember after you died
I used to see you
on the road
coming from the opposite direction

Was pretty sure it was you—
but you passed so quick,
it's something I've kept to myself
these twenty-five years

'til this Thanksgiving
sitting around the table with
Cousin Richard, he tells me that

he often sees *his* dad driving, so now
I'm wondering if you're on the same road
meeting up somewhere, maybe at the
bar just 'round some corner

buying Uncle Marshall a couple of beers
and betting on some football game.

JANE BUTKIN WAGNER

San Antonio, Texas, 1975

We were the only ones in the neighborhood
To have a tall wooden fence
With knotholes you could look through
And see outside the neighbor's chainlink
Heavy with honeysuckle and high
Feathery-headed weeds
Waiting to be cut down.

Marty Valdez used to scale our fence
And stare at my blond head.
For the touch of my hair
He'd offer me pink candy
And small porcelain cats,
But past his father's whistle
Nothing ever lasted.

Whistle, two fingers between the teeth,
And Marty'd be back over the fence and eating
Mexican food in his mother's crowded kitchen.
At my house, we ate the same, hot and strong
(But quiet) and it was different:

It was like my family
Slouching in the back of a mariachi mass
Turning red with the heat
And lost when the old priest
Slipped into Spanish.

Leslie Patterson

A Call to Duty

We were Hill Country folks
transplanted in San Francisco by war
and housed above Baker's Beach
in the Presidio Park apartments
with four children, a cocker spaniel

and one bath
compensated by a seductive view
of the Golden Gate Bridge.

Sometimes
our bed would wake us
with an unexpected little leap
and the dangling handles
on a cherry chest would
jiggle a brassy little tune.

Far out on the water deep
fog horns would sound
their spectral refrain

hoooo . . . hoooo . . . hoooo . . .
You would stir

and once still half in sleep
you deigned to opine
Someone should feed the cows.

MARY-AGNES TAYLOR

Us Yankees

My first day teaching in Texas,
An eighth grader said to me,
It's okay to be a Yankee, Sir.
My mother's a Yankee.
She's from Arkansas.
When no no else laughed,
I just said, *I'd like to meet her.*
Us Yankees like to stick together.

DAVID J. THOMPSON

Tejas

It is a land so long and broad and rich,
    So ripe with what the good earth gives to man,
That settlers came to crisscross and to stitch
    A quilt of habitations. They began
At rivers east and south, and from the sea;
    Soon spread into the valleys, woods, and plains.
They brought sharp tools and oiled weaponry;
    They worked and fought and slowly made their gains.

Their footholds, dug in stubbornness and strife—
    The river fords and trading posts and forts—
Soon grew into the synapses of life,
    Connecting all the inland needs with ports
Receiving merchandise, machines, and men.
    The fallow ground was plowed, the ranches grew:
A mix of races came together when
    The rising glory of the state was new.

Its history, a bold adventure tale;
    Its natural resources overflow;
Its spirit like the fiercest winter gale,
    Or like the gentlest zephyr that may blow.
But here is where the greatness really lies:
    In open hearts, as free as prairie wind;
And courage that is wide as western skies;
    And being Texan means being a friend.

James O. Dobbs

Defiant Conqueror of Texas Prairie

to my grandfather John Wesley Roberts (Beanpaw)

The wooden plow cut furrows
of blackened sod as sharply as
faces' features were chiseled
by prairie winds, piercing sun.

Thickly grown eyebrows shaded
deep-set eyes and goatee
distinguished his face.

Row after row stretched behind him
and mule Molly as their day's work
proceeded slowly, evenly.

Distended veins ran blue rivers
under his skin, in rough hands
as they gripped plow's handles
and held sturdy cut.

He etches a tall lean
walking silhouette
in memory.

PEGGY ZULEIKA LYNCH

Local Culture

Half a mile off the Interstate,
a Czech bakery is still
the place for local
conversation

about noninvasive
cancer treatment in central
Texas. But the excitement
at the new Czech Inn on I-35 is

all about the promise
of McDonald's. Kolache
with poppy seed, the favorite, they
tell me, of the old folk, tastes faintly

like a memory of Prague.

STEVEN SCHROEDER

Weeding the Family Plot

Something in your genes
that sets your office hands
to feeling dirt.

That sets your heart
on the rusted tendrils
of barbed wire.

Waiting for a cloud's fist,
waiting for a south wind.

My ancestors prayed for rain
in their years of drought,
prayed for the abolition of debts,
the souls of the dying.

Paid no attention to their brown skin
coated with a fine red dust
and furrowed on the back of their necks.

Just like the lizards
that crawl with certain impunity
on their aging headstones.

Ken Wheatcroft-Pardue

Class Line

There's enough to go around
but only just.
Our long-ago primate promise
to store grain in jars
to raise the girl babies
to walk so's everybody could keep up
means some of us live
right next to the cracks
jostled, hanging on

like only white trash can.
And when you settle, take a break,
when you just throw out that mess, it's
been sitting too long,
impossible to clean,
when you say
"She knows the score, I'm not
really hurting anyone"
I'm telling you, no lie,
everybody has to scoot over
and one of us
one of *us*
loses the room to stand
slides from desperate, cramping arms
and vanishes.

MAGGIE JOCHILD

Los Muertos

They wait for us to come
Perfectly still in their satin-lined boxes
Only the slightest creaking of bones
This is the day, they think,
Of paper roses,
Melting candle wax,
And the slight scent of *canela*
A day of singing,
Beautiful sound of babies cooing
And children laughing
Of leaves dancing overhead
The wonderful feel,
The oh-so-miraculous feel
Of saltwater tears,
Seeping through *tierra*
A salve on dry, dry bones

NANETTE GUADIANO-CAMPOS

PARED TO THE HEART

A gift of pears pares my memories to one:
my grandfather dragging a lifeless leg down

the steps of the house he built, thumping
his cane in the dirt past the barn he raised,

to the orchard heavy with plums, pears,
and apples. I stand under his stroke-stricken

arm and push up with all my six-year-old
strength toward a perfect pear above his head.

      Then jump back.

The dead arm falls to his side and snaps
the stem as he teeters, crippled fingers gripping

the pear like a newly-hatched heart. But I know,
a pear never returns to the branch as a blossom.

                CAROLYN A. DAHL

GOOD OL' BOY

Landed in D.C.
After a stint in Nam,
Ever a son of Texas.
Strode state-named streets
In cowboy boots,
Rusty curls poking
From his Stetson,
Belt buckles the
Size of fried eggs.
Drank coffee from a chipped mug,
Chowed down on three-alarm chili.
Given to expressions
That require some translation,

"Grinnin' like a mule
Eating briars through
A picket fence," he'd say.
Hands tough as leather,
Heart soft as kid skin,
Pierced by trials and hardships
He was raised not to talk about.
After a year, bothered by
Urban bustle and bitter cold,
Climbed into his pickup
And headed for El Paso.
Last I heard, still a
Tender-hearted loner
In search of a time long gone.

Ann Reisfeld Boutté

Missing the Point

Your guitar nests at our feet on the porch,
persists in lulling me with strings now still.
You take a long, slow draw from your pipe,
pointing across the road with your other hand.
Not following the suggested target,
my eyes focus instead on your extended finger,
the manicured curve of your nail allowing
it to slide off a *G* string as easily

as it glides across my ribs when the moon is full.
I study the smooth cuticle, the hair now white
across knuckles buckled by the journey.
You ask if I can see it, there in the meadow,
slipping through the sunset's shadow.

I wonder at the distance between
that finger and what you want me to see,
see only what I need.

Anne Schneider

An Inconvenient Condition

Narcolepsy
can cause one to fall abruptly into sleep,
especially when strong emotion
strikes too sharply or too deep

like the seven frisky puppies
caught on film at dinnertime
who ran toward overflowing bowls
but halfway there,

excited, fell into sleep.
Moments later, they woke,
ran, became excited,
fell, slept again.

Emotion
rarely pushes my wake/sleep button,
but each time I try to write about
my deepest feelings since you've gone

I wake
to find the clock's hands
have moved on.
And my poems remain inside.

Marilyn Stacy

Skinny Girl from Nacogdoches

Crystal has knife scars
on her throat where
a boyfriend cut on her

She lives down the hall,
but says she won't stay
in Houston very long

When she uses our phone
she whispers into it

Tells us she's afraid her ex-husband
may come looking for her,
the one who burned her house down

Crystal uses his last name
just to throw him off,
says he'd never think she still would

Once when we called her
to the phone, her face went
white but it was alright,
only her Ma up in East Texas

Crystal's country accent thickened
as she talked to the folks back
home, "Love ya, love ya," she kept
saying, her voice loud and pretty,
her scars and terrible secrets
all but forgotten

KEDDY ANN OUTLAW

THE COURTHOUSE SQUARE REGULARS

Ancient trees enclose the courthouse square.
Beneath them, old men hunch on a low stone
boundary wall. They study passing cars,
passersby, farm trucks, birds and sky.
Sun is their clock, moving them hour
by hour from shine to shade. Sometimes
they talk, remembering past wars.
Mostly they sit. They spit. They stare.

JEAN H. MARVIN

Big White Car, Big White Hair

Claws curled
around
the steering wheel,
she wields
the lumbering
tonnage,
claims
the passing
lane,
never yields
to smaller
dustier autos.
They tailgate
and swerve,
dart
and withdraw.
She sees
them, if
she notices,
as fluttering
annoyances,
steel
moths in awe
of her great,
horizon-blocking
glare.

Suzanne Blair

II. What's Next in Eden: Texas Flora & Fauna

Cottonwood Lullaby

It wasn't the ancient piano in one dark corner
of the parlor, Grandmother's only allowed luxury
bought decades before for fifteen hard-earned dollars
of precious egg money, a dollar a month until paid
in full. After an endless day of canning and cooking
for field hands working, tired fingers lovingly
caressed its yellowed keys into a heartfelt, though
out-of-tune rendition of "Amazing Grace," accompanied
by equally off-key voices making a joyful noise.

Nor was it the mean-spurred, raucous rooster's
pre-dawn bugle-call serenade closely followed
by daily predictions of weather and hog future
fluctuations—static sputtered across indifferent
air waves warming into another sizzling sunup.

By day, it was a common cottonwood,
gnarled and worn, releasing its silk-like seed
puffs downy and white, just right for robin-
nest linings or a child's plaything—and a nuisance
to be swept off the front porch by overworked adults.

But evening brought its magical transformation:
as the whippoorwill's plaintive call softly rang
across midsummer's wild-rose hills, twilight's
cooling breeze stroked the ancient
cottonwood's love-shaped leaves, creating
a lullaby like the pitter-patter of softly
falling rain—to carry a weary
household quietly off to sleep.

Sheila Tingley Moore

Mockingbird

(Mimus Polyglottos)

No wonder you were made gray.
Decent but not sensational.
Oh, larger and with better posture
than say, a humpbacked quail—
sure, nice white military stripes.
We can't grant you
more pulchritude than that.

Singing? That's another story.
Your notes pour out
in rainbows, canyons, technicolor.
Rhythms? Rat-a-tat, ragtime, staccato.
Your songs like fractal geometry—
all over the place,
God doing riffs.

Jan Seale

From a Reluctant Shut-in to a Confirmed Recluse

The birds notice first, talking it up among themselves
In dialects of bird talk that differ regionally.
It criss-crossed my mind
Like a flock of fractious grackles
How terribly quiet it would be
If the birds all left suddenly.

In my currently depressed and wingless state,
I could not hope to simulate
Their timeless flight across the sky—
These earthbound words
As close as I can come
To their more exuberant medium.

Joe Blanda

Valley Orange

Crying out "Pick me up!
Peel me! Eat me!" like a
person with an attitude,
wanting to be noticed, then
pulled apart and made appealing,
sucked dry of all aspirations,
savored with wild abandon.

Betsy Slyker

Sightings

The wolf crouches like a sphinx
on a cliff above a pond & hiking trail,
her gray pelt & perked ears gleaming
steel in the sun, legs ready to pounce,
as her gold eyes scan her territory.
The intruder hears her howl once. Sends
a 5000-volt chill through him. Suddenly a rustle
in the reeds. A great white heron catapults
like a water angel to heaven. Wolf vanishes.
Vultures appear on live oak, draped in black
shining armor, their sharp beaks yawning
between meals. Next curve, the intruder
eyes an anhinga spreading his white-streaked
wings wide as Texas, sunning himself
on a boulder after gorging. Intruder stops
at a dying sycamore alive with skylarks
puffing their brown chests as if posing.
Startled by their boldness, intruder drops
walking stick, squints at glistening mushroom
domes shading turtles, as he retrieves it.
What's next in Eden? He wonders,
Sunday morning.

Gerald R. Wheeler

Bandera

Larking about on the southerly breeze
they carry the sudden ache of the world,
one, two, two more, then four monarchs streaming—
October's compass colliding with air.

From our deck we watch an orange bunting
funnel through Texas without North star, guide.
Butterflies masted to music, impulse
of invisible iambs, recurring.

Let every beat of each tiny wing
be our essay in constancy.

Joy Palmer

In Season

Tormented during
an autumn drive
turning tear-shot eyes
toward the window
she locks glances
with another hollow gaze—
a deer draped over
the bed of a rusty truck
blood-smeared nose
broken twig legs
dangling beside
a crated bitch
quivering and slobbering.

She sees herself
in miniature
dwindling within
their fixed stares.

SuzAnne C. Cole

Texas Greater Fritillary

a butterfly! a flash
of brown and bone
silver fritillary underwings
fanning light around my feet

i sit on paving stones
and watch it preen
dark antennae quivering
in examination of my flesh
pale hair-thin tube extending
to siphon up what moisture
could be found between my toes

an impulse to catch it
flits past, unused
instead, i watch till
wings and wind carry it away
in a perfect mix of curves and line
thinner than the finest paper
lighter than my breath
more delicate
than any word I know

Deb Akers

Tumbleweed

frets through the green
growing years
dreams of the end
the shift to brown
breaks loose
takes its seed load
starts rolling
towards the answer

Anthony Russell White

THE INTENSITY OF FLOWERS

Up from the cool dark soil
pierce green tips of bulbs,
stalks lift up buds that blossom into flowers,
lifting the low-slung ground into
bursts of stolen sun,
some bright before the foil of earth,
some suspended high, spangling the air.

Form your lips around syllables
that name their blatant invitation.
Feel what it means to bloom,
say *a flower.*
Say *yellow* and feel your mouth go round.
Consider the perfect
gold of coreopsis, daisy, daffodil.
Say *exfoliation* and feel the triggered coil of blooming.
See them beckon, say their names before they're gone.

Say *blue* like a lover's kiss. *Blue*
is the longest word of one syllable,
it melts in rapture
like the last limber ice.
Do you see the iris light up like a flame,
feel her veined tissues cool the air at noon?
Imagine her single, perfect moment.
Go see the flax petal's one day.
Rise early, one morning, before it's gone.

Hummingbirds bow at altars in my garden,
glean the living fire of flowers.
And I follow, catching words
like emerald spiders on carnations,
plucking blossoms,
singing songs.

SHEARLE FURNISH

El Árbol Milagroso

On the way to *el árbol milagroso*
the young girls told stories *del otro lado*

like a brush with the spirits through
a window over the washer and dryer.

Turo's sister laughed as she drove
over vanishing pools on hot asphalt,

when unexpected a bristle of javelinas
appeared grazing the dry *kiñena* ditch.

Pale plastic Jesus fixed to the dash,
cardboard signs and suspicion led

past the weeping Virgin's water-tank,
past the dead snakes hung on a rail,

to a fence laced with sun-faded garlands,
to a cross studded with glinting *exvotos*,

guarding the Jerusalem olive tree,
bound in burlap and colored ribbons

protecting the saint from pilgrims
with pocketknives and prayers.

Mira—she led us to the shrouded trunk,
planted her ear against its skin, sighed—

oye—eyes closed. Next, inside I
listened as the waterfall laddered sky

to ground, through the live green core
so far from what we thought we knew.

Katherine Durham Oldmixon

Almost the Same Thing

At dusk, I walk a back road on the island
where wheel ruts overgrown with grass
slice through the brush and T into the paved road.
A young coyote runs toward me.
He isn't traveling fast, just purposefully.

We both freeze.
An instant before, I had been thinking about imagination
or rather my lack of it;
he, by the look of his rib cage and the hollow
pit of his stomach, hunger.

Seconds pass.
We stand looking at one another.
I turn away first. Then the coyote turns and disappears
into the dark undergrowth.

Carol K. Cotten

Voyagers

*"caught up in a tropical storm
that moved across the Atlantic"*
The Birds of Texas, *by John L. Tveten*

in a far field
dotted with cows
I see cattle egrets
like white commas
at the hooves of each
bovine sentence

when they flap up,
not long, at the slow
lowing heads,
they're startling ivory
apostrophes

and when I imagine them—
storm-tossed, a turmoil
and plummet of long legs
and plumage in the
roaring dark—

I see a whole new grammar
aflutter across the atlantic
bound for a simpler life,
the shade beneath cows

Jim LaVilla-Havelin

Waxwings

We waited all year for the passover
of the cedar waxwings. They fly north
on their pilgrimage over the Hill Country
then on to the Great Lakes.

Winter visitors—we could mark off the days
until they congregated in the pecans,
their thin song like choir boys
before their voices have broken.

But this year a wave of warm weather in March
confused everyone. Berries swelled on the ligustrum—
and like a font, the birdbath overflowed,
but the waxwings never came.

We dreamed of waxwings,
their gold-tipped tails, their crested cloaks,
then we awoke to find the trees stripped of fruit.
Some lay crushed and bleeding
on the ground, but the air was silent,
the waxwings gone.

Sally Alter

Willow City Wildflowers

We went in search of bluebonnets,
fields of blue peppered with paintbrush,
a complement of oranges and blues.

The day stayed gray; the fields, muted.
The sky, too, was void of color,
everything gray as miles and miles of asphalt.

We scouted the hills, scoured the roadsides,
spotted ochre lichen on speckled granite,
tiny white flowers clumped among cacti.

Finally we spied some premature bonnets—
no more than ten—our excitement as keen
as though we'd found a whole field.

We came too early, by maybe two weeks,
disappointing, yet somehow fulfilling.
The sweetest rewards are the most elusive.

Scott Wiggerman

Still Life With Chickens

It was that really cold snap we had winter before last
We brought the chickens into the house for the night
They eventually adjusted to the linoleum, but still
Preferred to cluster under the piano—no hawks
Could get through that piano. You kept reading
Even as I took flash pictures of the chickens, you
Loved your books. But when I put down the camera
And slid in beside you on the futon, for warmth and
A body in back of me as I watched the chickens
Then, then you forgot about the book. How can it
Be that it is all gone, not just the house and the piano
But the fuse and heat, the will to gather such things

Together and call them ours? Nobody knows what
It was like to be us then, not the chickens and not
You anymore, you have made a sacrament of for-
Getting. It is just me, like it was just me who got up
After we had fallen asleep and put down a bowl
Of water, a plate of barley, underneath the piano.

MAGGIE JOCHILD

EROS

Fingers sinking deep in dirt,
that trill of current
humming along tips and capillaries.
Digging for my self,
down in that moist earth.

Once the hollow is carved out,
the Surefire tomato finds her niche.
"Plant it deep," he said,
"All the way up to the first real branching.
That way there will be lots of roots,
lots of roots to withstand the extremes of Texas."

I feel as if I am covering bone of my bone,
flesh of my flesh.
Such a peculiar tenderness
in placing the plant just so,
gently heaping soft mounds,
blanketing with cariño and humus.

Tomato scent rises like incense,
prayer sprung from this simple act.
Stooping down to earth,
touching those fertile grains
that at the end will receive me
with gentle blanketing care.

MARY C. EARLE

Texas August

summer oak's too green here in Texas,
jasmine's grown wild, comes into the house
through cracks you can't even see,
tendrils nosing their way in

you don't know if it is benign
or malignant, this power
that unfolds into a question mark
and snakes up the wall

and you pull it away, pull it off
but you don't get to the caulk
and here it is back again,
palest tiny leaves at the end

darker shiny ones further down
and it will take over everything,
the house a fairy tale castle
woodcutter hacking away, just bones inside

and you think of getting the axe yourself
and you think of just lying back in it,
letting it rise around you like a cloud,
a cushion of green sleep

Janet McCann

Bee Creek

I spread my soul, and welcome summer in,
And sprawl beneath a brilliant, red-orange sun.
I listen to the Pedernales run,
And sluice, and slice, past cypress trees.
Heat—thick and turgid—whispered lilts of breeze,
The sonorous cicadas' buzz and drone,
The heady scent of onions, wild-sown—

Sharp spears of scrub grass prick my salty skin.
Out in the river, an unyielding rock
Refuses to erode with granite will.
And perched upon the surface of this block
A mockingbird is preening with her bill.
Abruptly, now she lifts her voice in song—
Bestows her benediction, and is gone.

MARTHA KIRBY CAPO

LOST LIGHT

A firefly buzzes the dark bush,
a sequin of lost light. Years
have passed since I held one.
Hands cupped, I catch the flying star,
curl my fingers around it like a tiny
church protecting a holy relic.

Inside the dome of skin, the firefly
glimmers. Greenish Morse-code
light flickers through locked fingers,
reminding me of old movies taken
when children owned the night.
How we raced barefoot through wet
grass, chasing bobbing lights
with out-stretched hands for traps.

None of us knew that abundance
would disappear with childhood, or
that fireflies wouldn't always come
with night. So without malice,
we squashed some lights, rubbed
iridescent juice on arms, flapped
pretend wings to telegraph the moon
that soon we would rise from safe backyards,
and return fallen stars to the sky's great height.

CAROLYN A. DAHL

Coyotes

for Gary Snyder

Coyotes approach. They howl
shadows of moonlit edge.

Inside their upturned song
opens a well of rising water.

At last it fills and they fall quiet.
That wild long slide into the dark,

splash of silence.

Cyra S. Dumitru

Freeing the Fireflies

I confess—it was I with a twist of wrist
who let go a tangle of fire,
freed the prisoners of the mayonnaise jar.

Freed them to dance their mating dance,
their arcing parabolas,
their upside-down tears.

Freed them to shine like cellophane
as they rose on warm thermals
above cirrus and ether.

To rise to the vast dark of space
where a pair of Gemini astronauts
will spot them drifting
past their half-moon windows,
like a constellation yet uncharted.

Ken Wheatcroft-Pardue

The Mare

Pregnant with her first set of twins, past due,
she rambles through the clover sans a care.
The twins are restless, frolicking
in the warm, dark meadow of her womb,
kicking her placenta to the brink
of tearing. She pays them no mind,

as if, basking in the glow of horse sense,
she knows the time will soon come
when she'll lie down on the straw
of her stall in the barn, roll over
on her side, squeeze them one by one
to glory in a shaft of sunlight,

devour their gleaming afterbirth, nudge them
to the thin, wobbly stilts of their legs,
suckle them till she's wasted, and turn them,
each on his own sweet time, out
to the thankless pasture of freedom,
all without the hindrance of a thought.

LARRY D. THOMAS

Cactus

Cactus
Raises thorny fingers
To the sky
Pulling down
The pastel colors
To pin them,
Briefly,
To the distant
Mesa.

JERRI BUCKINGHAM HARDESTY

Grackle at Spring Wedding

He sits on the roofline,
a South Texas gargoyle,
his flat boat-tail stiff behind him
like a sail holding him steady
in the undertow
of a heavy Gulf wind.

Spewing his gravelly remarks
in the rude jargon
of a street corner Casanova,
black hair slicked back,
tight pants pulled up high
to tuck in his ridiculous shiny shirt,
he is a nuisance
to well-mannered folks.

Always on the make,
a perpetual bag of hot air,
the epitome of tackiness,
he ignores the solemn ceremony
taking place below.
A party crasher, a home wrecker,
he is apt to speak up loudly
instead of forever holding his peace.

Even with his constant intrusions,
we allow his presence,
admire his spunk,
offer him as proof
that God has a sense of humor
and knew just the bird
to send to Houston.

Anne McCrady

Pelicans

She had never seen so many

There was the lone bird
which circled around the docked ferry
and the small flock
which vied with cormorants
for the piers on the west bank

And on their drive
they were everywhere
flogged by squalls
lumbering across the road
like wounded bombers
trying to stay aloft

Under the drawbridge
where the gales tore at the wipers
slapped at the roof
rushed under the car's carapace
like a weight lifter intent on turning it over
they had gathered
a milling crowd in a shallow pond

On the way back
the outline of a gutted pelican
on the pavement
its buff crest and wing feathers
attempting a take-off in the wind

And then the excitement
of watching one get off the ground
so close

MARCELLE H. KASPROWICZ

Fritiniency

Katydid, cricket, beetle,
grasshopper in wild oats—
melody of midsummer's night.

And in the air
a calligraphy of mosquitoes,
male and female,
a green-black, stylized cloud

scrolled over stagnant water
whining and whining
a high-pitched monotone.

Susan Terris

Totem to a Dying Breed

dedicated to Clyde Roberts, rancher

He killed it with his pickup in 1940
while it was intent on disemboweling a kid
in the middle of a Schleicher County pasture.

wing span 7'1"

It had taken one or two angoras a week since
they had started to drop in late January, and
by March he had lost more than twenty of the flock.

body weight: 37#

He and the boys wrapped the wings in baling wire
and took it to the taxidermist in a little town
down the road, where it was mounted—wings outspread.

genus: Aquila

Years later it was donated to a Girl Scout camp and,
as most things, forgotten by the sons until they reached
their own majority, had sons, and began to reminisce.

    species: crysaetos

The youngest son went through McCamey a few years back,
stopped off at the aging camp, was surprised to find
it still maintained by the original caretaker in her eighties.

    sex: mature male

Now it hulks above his mantle, commands the peaceful den
with an agate eye, feathers slightly dusty, in need of grooming,
razor beak fixed in perpetual scream.

    est. Texas pop.: 100

Carol Cullar

Upon Leaving Galveston Island

Before I forget, let me tell you how to get to the coral beans. You must
see them. Go in the early morning in spring when the fog still lies low to
the ground. Take Stewart Road west from 61st Street. Turn right on 99th,
left on Schaper, and right onto 103rd. There will be pastures on your right
and left. Travel up the road to the stable made from pieces of cyclone
fence, boards, and tin. On the way you may see the brown mare's halter
still snagged on the barbed wire fence. By the gate is a huge lantana with
orange and yellow flowers. However, it's not there that I want you to
look. Turn around. Across the road is a scruffy oak beside a gate guarded
by a mountain laurel. The oak hasn't been trimmed in years and you can't
see its trunk. The coral beans are behind that oak. Be prepared. They
rise up like red-roofed Chinese temples high in the mountains outside
the Forbidden City. You might even hear the gong calling the monks to
morning prayer.

Carol H. Cotten

Westlake Deer

Heavy with kid the doe,
who lifted the heads off
200 pansies last night,
browses along the rocky incline
munching fresh sprouts
the sometime rain has raised.

Neighbors know and brake
to near halt, watch them
amble heavily, unconcerned
from ditch to the deer run opposite.

Drivers unfamiliar with this S-curved
meandering two-lane, hunting an address,
dash headlong only to cripple and
leave them to die slowly.

A gathering of buzzards, smell of
carcass decaying, another decimation
in our urban neighborhood
where lots are left rough and rocky
pandering neglect.
Deer like it that way.

Kaye Voigt Abikhaled

Wild Mustangs

A man said to me, "You know you're half woman, half boy and half hound dog." I told him that those were probably the reasons I loved being a film scout.

Journeys were my joy. In my camera bag were two cameras, a reporter's notebook, tons of film and a roll of toilet tissue.

I got lost a lot. That was the best part. On the Tall Grass Prairie Preserve outside Pawuska, Oklahoma. In the maple syrup woods of Moosehead,

Maine. Under the open skies of Blackhills, North Dakota, where once I almost stayed.

Dayton Hyde lived there. A John Wayne of a man who loved horses enough not to ride them. He lived in a trailer house on a fifty-thousand acre sanctuary for eighteen hundred wild mustangs he'd taken from feedlots in Arizona and New Mexico so that they wouldn't become dog food. Some he called by name. Magnificent Mary, Golf Balls, Funny Face, Shaggy Roan, and wild as they were they came.

I took a picture of Dayton standing on a hilltop as the sun went down, wearing faded jeans and a new leather jacket and holding a lasso that he never used on horses in his huge hands. Suddenly, the rope went around me and he pulled it the same way I used to pull on a string of bacon while crabbin'.

When I got on the plane to return to Texas my heart hurt and for a moment I didn't think of the man I was engaged to. I thought of getting off. But I didn't. I thought of the mustangs running out and beyond our small stations in life head-first into a world ruled by nature and wished that I was wild.

KATIE OXFORD

ALL SOULS

Murmuration.
Across the rice fields
small dark birds of no name I know
lift as one swirling body, to wheel
easily, a smoky mass expanding,
compacting, rounding into shadow
clouds. Shifts blur the edges,
but not one bird wisps away
or trails behind. Fierce energy
drives this wave, shapes
the constant fluid change.

TRUDY S. GUINEE

Fishing Frustrations

I wanted to catch a really big fish
to impress my newfound friend.
With bated breath and baited hook
I set out to contend
with catfish, perch, croppie, bass—
anything to prove my skill.
Showing how it was done in August sun
was a matter of wit and will.

My skin burned. My minnows boiled.
My reel fell off my rod.
I stuck a hook in my hand. I thought,
"There is no God."
My friend reeled in a three-pound bass
on only her second try.
I sat in pain and agony
as I watched her first fish fry.

Lois U. Chapman

Heirloom Hocked

I always gathered
spring greens
with Gram

down by Mission Creek

we would climb
those steep banks
picking
dock
dandelions
lamb's quarter
sheep sorrel
poke weed
and nettles

using knowledge
handed down
from mother to daughter
from England and Ireland

now with Gram dead
and a mother who was too busy
I've become uncertain
can't quite
remember

how many times do I boil the poke
and was it the leaves or the berries

SHERYL L. NELMS

A Collared Peccary by Any Other Name

      would still be a javelina,
would deserve no respect
some say, because
it has borrowed
the shape of pig
hide of wolf
hackles of porcupine
smell of skunk
bark of dog
rattle of snake.

So what's a poor javelina to do
to gain points in personal charm?

These are its favored things:
one elegant necklace of white,
two babies cherubic,
three curious toes on the hind feet,
and numberless prickly pear salads.

JAN SEALE

frost on the cedar—
chickadee
warming up its throat

Nancy Kenney Connolly

At Home in Southeast Texas, July

When the rains flashed, we ran for the oak
and stood near its massive trunk
in the massive dark, and after a while,
remembered how our great-grandmother said
she played here as a girl, how one day
a man came to find the age of the tree,
and how everyone was surprised to learn
it was older than grandma's grandma's grandma,
older even than that.

It bowed its back to the driving wind,
its feet clawing earth in a mighty hold,
its leaf-on-leaf pattern a thatch to keep
us dry. We watched limbs lift and swing
as we stood in the great inverted bowl
they made, while time raged around us.

A live thing, its bloodlines anchored here
deep as our own family lines. Generations
flowed between us as we waited, the tree's
arms holding us like an ancient mother's.
And I thought, what time itself
has kept, we must keep.
So God help him who comes with axe and saw,
God help him who comes with winch and chain,
God help anyone who thinks to take this tree
which sheltered those who came before,
century after century
and shall hold those who are to be.

Violette Newton

cats & dogs

Murdoch slept through all night yips and yawns
of a half dozen bluetick hounds

not-so-country grandboys woke constantly,
yipped ourselves across cold Saltillo tile floors

it's the noise stirs them, grandpa said, mockingbirds,
avocados thumping on the hard valley dirt,
rustle of leaves, nothing but scaredy-cat old dogs

it's the smell that wakes them up, woke him up

he'd shot a jaguar once, hounds bawling in the Tamaulipas
cloud forest dim, cat after a new milk calf tied to a post

revolution drove the cats south, Murdoch north barely
four dog generations ago

one night, June of '66, when the blues let loose
he was up with a 12-gauge before we could
wipe the dirt from our eyes, watch through the
kitchen window as he stalked the barnyard

an *oncillo*, he thought, looking for chickens, just a guess
he chunked at us that night, or maybe a bobcat,
gato del monte, he called it, stalking the peahen in the pecan

the next morning wisdom ran with the guineas

grandpa couldn't find the tan kid goat or an excuse,
nor explain the footprints by the barn, size of pancakes

no missing that look on his face, we'd seen it a thousand
times in that picture of him at twenty with that jaguar hanging
next to two old hounds

tony gallucci

Dancing

See! A piñon branch,
partnering the wind.
Catch a circling fly,
buzzing in the sun.
Look: a loosened leaf,
waltzing in the wood.
Mate your hand with mine,
move your feet in time.
Everything will dance
when it has a chance.

Geneva Fulgham

Precursors

In Central and South Texas,
hot, passionate,
pink redbud blossoms
peek out early,
while it's still chilly.

Their flowers
more strikingly colorful
because they sneak up
on us unashamedly—
next to dead trees,
bushes, brown grasses.

They flaunt
the freshness
of their adolescence,
reaching out
between death
of winter
and new birth
of spring.

The surprise
of their colors
speaks to us,
reassures us
of endless,
soon-coming,
sun-warmed,
nowhere-but-Texas
seasonal days.

BARBARA YOUNGBLOOD CARR

When We Brought the Tree Limbs Down

It was nothing more than a burning reflex
of muscle and bone and dare-you-to-climb-higher.
Mother had said her hydrangeas weren't getting
any sun and what could we boys do about it?

We were fools, trying to saw, and swing,
and lift more than we should. We were
sharp axes and imbalanced ladders and
watch-out's and weight on dead branches.

But finally, it was us on the ground,
sawn branches, and all boys, safe and sound.
We said oh and ah and feel that sun
and my, won't those hydrangeas grow now?
We pounded each other on the back,
stretched imaginary suspenders, said good job.
Mother cooked a huge supper.
We went to bed full of food, bravado, and sawdust.

And did not sleep. A wind came through
that night. It curled over the absent limbs
like a lost tooth. It wondered. It searched.
It sang a mournful song we did not want to hear.

ALAN BIRKELBACH

The City Girl's Regret

A friend's ranch in April—pasture of prairie
wildflowers—sprawling verbena, red-yellow
gallardia, fleabane daisy's threadlike flowers.
I walk the creek, gentle spill of waterfalls
singing, longing to strip off designer jeans,
stiff shirt, wade naked into the water.
But I'm not alone.

I climb a hill into the woods, nibbling
stalks of sour wood sorrel, sick with
unforeseen envy, desiring the bitterweed
nestling in caliche to flower just for me,
the madrone tree guarding the summit
to be my tree, mine alone.

I want to stand here as proud possessor
of all I survey . . . but I'm not.
I chose differently.

SuzAnne C. Cole

Fireflies

Fireflies are born into flight.
Into the light of their bodies they come
Bearing gifts from the world of sky,
Possibilities we, earthbound, can only dream.

Into the light of their bodies they come
Sparkling, sparking imagination, creating lives,
Possibilities we, earthbound, can only dream
In pre-dawn hours not burdened by expectations.

Sparkling, sparking imagination, creating lives,
A man shows me what it means to fly.
In pre-dawn hours not burdened by expectations
He loves me with luminous freedom.

A man shows me what it means to fly.
Minutes in the sky become tiny stars of the night.
He loves me with luminous freedom.
Touching, we fly on once-in-a-lifetime wings.

Minutes in the sky become tiny stars of the night
Pitching themselves toward distant sisters.
Touching, we fly on once-in-a-lifetime wings,
Wandering home as though lightning-struck.

Pitching themselves toward distant sisters,
Bearing gifts from the world of sky,
Wandering home as though lightning-struck,
Fireflies are born into flight.

Lianne Elizabeth Mercer

War and Peace

Oh, how they flap
their midnight wings!
Oh, how they swell
themselves and screech,
harassing the sparrows,
pecking each other,
voraciously snatching
seeds from the feeder,
>while
>on
>a
>nearby
>rooftop,
>a solitary
>dove
>silently
>waits
>his
>turn.

Lounell Whitaker

Blazing fields flicker
with Indian paintbrushes
   the color of flame.

MARY TINDALL

THE VERNAL POOLS AT ENCHANTED ROCK

Enchanted Rock can glisten like the head
of balding God on summer's rainy days
when sun comes after rain and brightly burns.
The steam flies up like haloed rings. It turns
the rock to church. Some crannies dodge sun rays,
become like holy night, less filled with dread.

The vernal pools where gaps have formed in rock,
steel-hard yet cleavage-prone, these small green lakes
eternally persist. This peaceful park
has taught pool creatures to adapt to dark,
evolve, become new species, and it takes
a special breeding space to grow strange stock

of gill-slit-breathing things not found elsewhere.
It takes this site so interestingly round
some people think it sanctified. This ball,
this rounded bit of granite grace, would call
to native folk. Enchanted Rock was found
and used by them for sacred worship. There

respect for God and what He could create
began to grow. The strange and hallowed fish
were praised. And now we see this rugged sphere
as birthing site for unique life. We hear
a peaceful breeze caress the rock and wish
to keep this plot as place for life innate.

J. PAUL HOLCOMB

Deep Red

Christmas afternoon. The gifts opened
and the wrappers burned, glitter gone
from all but children's eyes, I ride out
into the country with my brother.

Winter wheat glistens keen as fur
across the fields; the cattle are dreams,
the world a postcard mailed from far-
away—so we get out to read.

Armadillos everywhere—
opossum, crow, woodpecker, rabbit.
Hungover from last night, my brother
holds up a turtle shell as though

he's just won his first merit badge.
After war and divorce, we've come home
to look for bones and feathers in the sand
of a dry river. Cottonwoods stand guard.

I wonder at the blood between us,
how the open world contains
brothers and stars and armadillos—
the strange magnetics of love and hate.

Somewhere ahead, the crows are jabbering.
It's the owl telling them an old story
as light fails deep red
through the black tangle of trees.

Rawdon Tomlinson

Star jasmine blooming—
sweet heavy air drifting down
over small dead things.

SuzAnne C. Cole

Gadwall Duck Pond, West Texas

The bird lifts, slowly at first, feet dragging on the pond
but with powerful wing-beats breaks free
up and up and higher than the trees, yet circles round.
A single drop of water falls into the eclipse
of ripples that mark where he had rested; then he is gone.
The pond quiets. No touch of wind mars the glass
reflection of a chilling empty sky.
No echoes cross the silent shore.
It is early winter. Alone all autumn, he won't be back.

I've not been able to paint, write or even think.
I could chop another cord of logs
to stack beside the door before the flurries fall
or just give up, go home.
It's just so quiet. Can I make it through winter?
Maybe I should close the cabin. Sell it. Buy a single condo
in the city. Get a computer, TV, a telephone.

I reach for the paddle. Transfixed by a cry
beyond the trees, I hesitate, look up. He comes again
this time with another. A mate?
In the twilight of the cloudless sunset
they slice silently, splashlessly onto the pond,
swim close to my canoe,
call softly back and forth. Settle in.

So do I.

Mary Margaret Carlisle

Landscaping

a lawn mower roars
still poems go on above the whirr
or right below it

Dia VanGunten

Along the Railroad Track

We didn't think about the possibility
of snakes slithering among the density
of weeds, nor did we consider
the nettles there,

we only knew the sky was blue
and we were young and dewberries
were ready for reaping.

                              Lounell Whitaker

Cicadas

There's something George C. Scott
About a cicada, looking like a helmeted
Tank commander rolling inexorably forward,
Up and out of seventeen years underground,
Years of burrowing in darkness, of nursing
Sweet sap from swollen breasted roots, of
Isometric flexing and pumping hydraulic
Fluids beneath a brown-husked placenta
Carapace . . .

A diesel among insects, he buzz-rumbles
Up into my hardshell pecan, singing the
Dry hundred-degree evening for a moment's
Bliss, a moment's kiss of death, before tumbling
To the concrete, a file of ants marking the spot
Next morning as his lover prepares her eggs
For the allure of the cooling darkness.

Oh, armored harbinger, what new world
Will your children know, what new sun
Will rise in that time?

                              Jeffrey DeLotto

Summer with Mother

All day picking blackberries
the tender dark purple fruits
staining our fingertips
with their heavy juice
no matter how ginger the touch

from dawn to dusk to dark
until the whir
of gnats around our heads
became a ringing halo
we filled the bent metal buckets
we licked the sweat and juice
from our hands
watched the trickles trace new veins

at home there is a fire burning
we spill our pails
on the old wood table
talk of baking two hundred pies
our mouths stretch wide
our teeth shining like sapphires in the firelight

Toby Leah Bochan

The Grackle in His Black Silk Suit

It was the song, its consistent repeat
that drew me outside to discover the source—

a fancy flourish in a tux, a tiptoeing tenor,
a tease with dips and bows, a high wire act.

His apparent audience: the small lady in a front seat,
glimpsing the show while smoothing brown pleats

and me who stared silently, wiping hands on an apron
before sitting on porch steps to watch the show.

Mid-routine, the lady flew up an aisle, wing beats
brushing feather dust in my face as she raced by

as if to tell me that I could have him:
all he did was sing and dance, nothing more.

His intended gone, the tone changed to squawks
scolding me as if it was my fault she left.

MARGARET ELLIS HILL

LATE SUMMER IN TEXAS

They drop like jumbo gumballs
from the height of a great sycamore,
but arrive in only two colors:
washed-out green or worn-out brown.

Hard little bombs, they hit the roof,
then roll like bowling balls,
raucously down shingles and gutters,
or bounce like dimpled golf balls—
once, twice, sometimes more—
to land at last on the backyard deck.

Pricking bare feet if you step on them,
but remaining round and intact
with the mystery of alien space probes,
their spiny coats, like tiny sea urchins,
look menacing, impenetrable.

Once they crack they're pussycats:
soft, tan rabbit fur around a cherry-pit core—
more animal than plant—
wispy, ready to be swept by breezes
beyond the fence, beyond your life,
into a world that needs wonders.

SCOTT WIGGERMAN

CREPE MYRTLES

Those in full sun have
cracked open their round cases
and flounced out their ruffles,
their hot pink *vestidos*.
They sway under *el sol*—
whole bunches!—and unfurl their *fiesta* frills
from June to September.
We watch their salsas, their boleros,
their cha-chas, and my aunt shouts *"Mira!"*
every time we pass. And every time we pass,
they bob and curtsey, they twirl
their sizzling fringe.

This was my introduction to passion:
the flowers, the way they explode into
curls of crepe, and my aunt, the way
she soul-sings the old *canciones,*
right through drought,
through these long, tangled days after the accident,
sometimes through clenched teeth.
This is what I knew of spirit, *espíritu,*
that molten stream,
before I ever wrote a poem,
before it turned me inside out, like the blossoms.

REBECCA BALCÁRCEL

TEJAS IN BLOOM

Winecups:
      early sign of spring
      small claret petals braving
      highway adornment

Bluebonnets:
      hill country jewels
      lakes of lapis transforming
      tawny cow pastures

Bougainvilleas:
> tips of summer red
> leaves of winter green staging
> butterfly ballets

Chrysanthemums:
> shoulder corsages
> ribbon streamers proclaiming
> long live King Football

Poinsettias:
> altars banked with
> blooms red and gold heralding
> silent holy night

MARY-AGNES TAYLOR

YUCCAS AT 70 MPH

Spiked heads crown stout torsos
& shred the air,
an armless army in a permanent lean.
The Interstate splits their midst
near Van Horn
while they go about their ancient business
holding down the desert,
catching the tumbleweed runaways.
They bow to the breath
of the sun,
to what's been given them.

An 18-wheeler blows a hole
in the wind
and I follow it through, propelled
by the fool engine
of a restless heart.

SUZANNE FREEMAN

Alluvial Deposit

Between 1978 and 1997, twenty-two Columbian
mammoths were excavated near the Brazos River in Waco.
The skeletons are 28,000 years old. Adults were found to
be circling juveniles, possibly a group defensive position.
Two of the adults were trying to lift juveniles out of
danger. Scientists believe that the herd was trapped in a
creek bed by flood waters and buried in mud.

Under the tent
the scientist kneels,
examines the bones
twisted in layers
plastered in earth,
hears ghostly screams
of soon-to-be death,
imagines the matriarch
lifting the baby
toward grass and blue skies
until blood red waves
swept through the draw
knocked her aside
and into the muck;
he raises his brush
to whisper away
eons of silt
freeing the bones
and saving the baby
at last.

KAREN GERHARDT FORT

Hill Country

Even poppies pale
by willful daisies poking
through a cracked stone wall.

ANN REISFELD BOUTTÉ

Mockingbird's music
relaying another's song
   rises in the pines

MARY TINDALL

ASTERS

It must be October.
A solitary sunflower
is a hollow stalk,
rust and tire-black

in an unattended patch
between the tarmac plain
of a superstore lot and a bank.

There is beauty in neglect.
Move the buckled trolley.
Gather up deflated plastic bags.
There is not much litter.
Nobody walks anymore, remember?

You could sleep in there if you had to,
soft-shouldered
where the screams and sirens
and incessant blinking
traffic lights are muted.

Curl snake-like,
fetal-cosy
around silently choking goldenrods,

and let lilac clouds of aster stars
(lit by gas pumps' sodium glare)
fill midsummer night dreams
in the shadow of Halloween.

GRAHAM BURCHELL

SPRING AT WALLER CREEK

the body of the creek
did not notice the heron's foot

entering so cautiously—long gray nails
scaled ankle—without a ripple   and although

the water reflected every movement she made—
every cock of the head

quiver of long crest feathers—
the water could not be prepared   had no way

of reaching out a hand or even a word to stop
the piercing beak   the sudden loss

of the round silver fish
with red-rimmed gills who patrolled

one same circle of carefully sorted pebbles
these last many months waiting
for a perfect mate

ABIGAIL GREEN

APRIL IN PHARR

for Patty and Helmut

Wind lifts off the land:
Sunflowers take off
In all directions
Bougainvilleas ascend from trashcans
Palm fronds flutter above dusty streets
The neighbor's moonbounce
Tugs at its moorings.
Even the noontime siren
Floats up in an endless spiral.

Everything starts to fly:
Raptures of chacalacas
Aubades of whippoorwills
Parliaments of jays and green parrots
Golden-throated woodpeckers and kiskadees
Chirping on telephone wires
In grapefruit and olive trees
As they start the pilgrimage.

In the end, we all grow wings
Sprout bedraggled feathers
Just enough to lumber east
Toward the Gulf
Flapping awkwardly
Above the fields of levitating cabbages
Heading slowly toward a weighty world
Of clumsy pelicans
And punk-rock gulls.

CAROL COFFEE REPOSA

POSTMARK: AUSTIN, TEXAS

Hello from lupine land. Dispatched by web site
and urban myth, we wait beside the bridge
on Congress Avenue, thronged pilgrims come to see
those other mammals flying vampire night.
We've wandered over twilight's fraying edge
into sepia documentary:

the bats—a million plus—like winged monkeys
from Oz stampede from roosts and parapets,
uncoil like brown elastic lariats
that stretch and slither across the dusky
fur sky. The whir of wings. Arpeggios
of ultrasonic chords pin-prickle skin.
Flying dark the body pulses, chants in
the ancient tongue of ineffable Oh!

SUSAN J. ERICKSON

Coming-Out Party

We respond to the Park Ranger's invitation.
Embryos, removed from the sandy womb
of their birth mother to a surrogate's care,
are ready for their coming-out party.

She places a pile of hatchlings on Padre Island sand.
An infectious pile of wigglers,
sea turtle babes squirm
as if stimulated by pulsation of the sea

and the sound of gentle lapping.
A squadron of seagulls hovers,
veers and vies for dry cat food
tossed in the air by seashore staff.

Siblings nose heavy salt air, squiggle from the pile,
shove flippers into the sand, and drag themselves
toward foaming tongues licking at the shore.
The party crowd claps and cheers as the first wave

reaches the lead turtle, who rushes to follow
breaking bubbles. Ebbing tide pauses, gathers strength.
The next wave tumbles and thrashes the tiny creature
pulling from the beach into the unknown.

Virginia Frey

Axis

Not the long branch poised above my house,
but any leaf. Not the acorn plunking
along the shingles, but the jumping spider
tickling hairs on my arm. Not the stained-glass panel
floating against the window, but the waving lemon grass
pointing everywhere at once. How air wants
the smallest in us, while earth tugs

at the rest. The wasp on the curtain cannot sense this,
though the cat on the sill must, craning her neck,
plotting leap against fall, deciding not to move.
I lie on my side on the couch, glasses off,
open and close my eyes to the fuzz of the world.
What travels the edge of a leaf? What leaps free?
The oak beside my house stands tiptoe,
limbs extended, reaching. The cicada
lives in one world, then the next. Its brittle husk
clings briefly to the fence. Larger bodies
feel their gravity. How small before this stops?
The point where falling and flying are one.
Cattail fluff. Ash seed twirling. Feather down.

Ron Mohring

Rosemary

She doesn't seem to mind December.
Last week, despite the cold,
each branch burst
into tens of lavender blows

that brought the bees in droves.
They hover, light and fly
back legs packed saddlebags
of pale pollen, heather gray.

She didn't seem to mind the searing days
of summer, either. Fragrant blades
made stiff and prickly by the heat,
withered a bit, but stayed.

Then came the autumn rains.
She drank deep, and swelled,
then seduced us
with the glory of her smell.

Cindy Huyser

Freedom Rose

This yellow rose of Texas,
woven through a pristine white trellis
against my blue clapboard house,
would not be tamed.

It clawed its way toward the sun,
anchored its thorns on passing clouds.

Skillful pruning, even whacking—
all in vain.

I declared war
the day the rose broke the trellis
away from the house.
Yanked it, roots and all,
with my tractor,
moved it out by the windmill.
Let it sprawl there.

Next spring we sold the place.
One last look revealed
a thorny cane
snaking up beside the back door,
a single yellow rose
defying gravity.

Charlotte Jones

The Trickster

drought
along the back fence
the same gray-brown
    scruffy
    as the too-dry brush
after we rule out any
    kind of dog—

too skinny, too tall, too
  much like a wolf—
nagging at our minds like an
  animal gnawing on
  a meat-edged bone
comes the word, name, idea
  shaped around a trick
  and a wish, before it
  blends back into
  brown-gray deep brush
  without a trick
  or a sound—
coyote

     Jim LaVilla-Havelin

The Armadillo

Squish-squashing through the underbrush
through autumn leaves and brush
straight for the lonely road, and crossing it
determined, nothing fazed his strutting feet.

An armadillo made us brake hard by.
Ignoring husband's warnings I ran to spy
and picked him up by the sides of his shell
the firm, warm, pliant, upturned caravel.

Startled, his face reflected a measure of despair
at being lifted, inspected, stroked like a charmer,
his little claw feet still pumping in the air,
his ears, rolled cones sprouting under necked armor

of his crusted cylindroid, the little brute.
He was not pleased, that I could tell, but cute.
I let him down, he trotted off squish-squashing,
grumbling at the world's uneven flow and sloshing.

     Kaye Voigt Abikhaled

Airborne Fantasy

What if someone invented
a gossamer helicopter,

and what if each eye
could take a thousand
snapshots in all directions?

And what if it were an aircraft
that took off without effort,
glided, hovered, changed course,
like a flying saucer?

And what if it only made war
on mosquitoes?

What if it refueled its species
by love in tandem flight,
making us smile in envy?

What if we called it
Dragonfly?

Jan Seale

Cow Drinking

Lowing
& lowing
the cornfed beauty
strolled down
to the river
in a hide
both loose
& tight
evening's
wind streaming
out her spittle

so beautiful
stepping
in up to her
teats to drink
& dream
of drinking
the blurred
flowers of stars
awakening near
her great dark eyes

ROBERT BURLINGAME

FORGOTTEN BOUQUETS

Arranged around the tiny table
they wilt, too long
with too little.
They sway on long-stemmed stools,
sip wine, drink beer
in glasses, smoke
thin cigarettes.

They sow faded stories, tales
of what they'd do if
they had the time,
the money,
the man.

They plant hugs
stunted by moonlight,
perennial goodbyes,
dried seeds scattering
on sidewalks.

ANNE SCHNEIDER

Of Cows

then   there's the spacing   of cows
he takes it as an indication of something:

how sometimes they huddle—societal creatures
communities   of cows
            head to haunch
                  or
                        horns butting
and other times they spread themselves out across a field, still
chewing and re-chewing
bemused—if such creatures can be   bemused
space around them   like outfielders
room   enough   to   see   each   one

he is amazed, consistently amazed, by the spacing   of cows
randomness, deliberateness, an ambiguous mix of
intentionality   and   open space

it is in the space   between   cows
that the smell   of manure   rises
carried   on the breeze

it is in the space   between   cows
        that the sun   rises   sets
that the old trees take it all in—
    the sun   the cows   the birds   and even all these people
plunked down   haphazardly   in the middle
            of cows.

Jim LaVilla-Havelin

III. Between Here and the Horizon: Texas Places

When Texas No Longer Fits in the Glove Box

Once you unfold a road map of Texas, your world is changed.
Towns like Falfurrias, Carthage, and Maypearl suddenly become
part of your life and once you see them, you can't go back to
not knowing them. You *have* to go there, even if it's just
with your eyes—or your finger—tracing those
crow's feet county roads into unexplored territory.
That's how knowledge works. *That's* how knowing works.
Life is expanded; there's *no* going back.
There's no refolding the map.

It's like meeting an alarmingly charming man—
discovering his dangerous detours and thrilling new paths,
finding unforeseen forks and magnificent natural beauty.
You'll look up at him and know that the crinkly arch between his eyes
goes from Childress up to Amarillo, then back down to Muleshoe;
that the whites of his nails reach from Huntsville to Jasper;
that his green eyes encompass the metroplex—
from Ft. Worth to Denton to Dallas.

And you can't help but imagine that the crooked hairline
beneath his navel would run all the way down Highway 281,
and across the border, into dark, exotic Mexico;
or that his lips could take you on incredible road-trips
stretching clear across the state—from El Paso to Nacogdoches
with just a smile;
or that the best kiss of your life
would whisk you through the wild-flowered Hill Country,
and leave you weak-kneed and breathless
along the Riverwalk in old San Antone.

KARLA K. MORTON

A Very Personal Desert

It is so very dry here.
I shall die of thirst,
while those around me do not.

The opalescent lizard says,
"They drink tears to live,
tears from bottomless wells."

But how to find such places?
What maps might chart this region?
And do you know of a reliable guide?

Anthony Russell White

East of Amarillo

East of Amarillo the land is as flat as a griddlecake.
Between here and the horizon there is nothing.
Every direction reads the same: flat, dry, hot.
Maybe in the distance you can see the curve
as the earth reaches for the Piney Woods,
the Gulf coast, or rolling hills and prairies.
How can these plains sidle-up to Palo Duro,
red-rock canyon of song, sacred ground to some
who bargain for its return as rightful owners?
No one would argue for this land: flat, dry, hot,
sizzling on the skillet of July.
Even a boxcar far from the iron rails,
left with no place else to go,
stares empty-eyed, gape-mouthed,
from abandoned land.
The punch line from some sad joke
hangs on the boxcar's rusty, corrugated side:
"hay for sale." Hay isn't the only thing
folks aren't buying here.

Linda Banks

Silencio

In the Piney Woods,
you and I.

The shadow of a bird
or not a bird,
pale parchment leaves
impaled on nettles,
and a voice in my head sings
silencio, silencio, silencio.

The creek's hoarfrost,
shape of crystal toothpicks,
clusters near fallen logs,
ice sheaths drape themselves,
frozen cloaks over mute stones,
silencio, silencio, silencio.

On the trail large dogs bark,
their voices die
in blankets of crisp air,
brown-headed birds
with blue breasts
chatter in junipers,
flutter high, leaving us
silencio, silencio, silencio.

Wordless, I walk ahead of you
through beds of dying leaves,
earth's mettle to endure winter,
and now a boulder-strewn path
up to the waterfall
half frozen, still streaming.

Our communion floats
silencio, silencio, silencio.

MARTHA EVERHART BRANIFF

Luckenbach on Christmas

wind whistling at dusk
>beats Christmas lights on trailer
>>gypsy works magic

Sharman Speed

Palo Duro Canyon

The magic show begins
A few miles out of town
Makes high plains vanish
In thin air, pulls scarves
From sandstone hats
For twenty million years.
Gold and russet roar, red churns
On stones, blue hums in cottonwoods.
I never meet the conjurer
With all those colors up his sleeve
The sorcerer with boulders
In his hands, levitating caprock
Balancing an outcrop on his head.

I never hear his incantations
Dream instead of shades,
Almost see Georgia O'Keeffe
Scrambling up a hill, sketchbook
In her arms to paint some sensual poppy
All those epic flowers
Everything in motion swaying
Past the names designed
To keep them still: Sad Monkey, Goodnight,
Lighthouse, Prairie Dog Town.
I see it all, believe,
Before the artist finally escapes
Leaving just the props.

Carol Coffee Reposa

Secret

So the Canadian girl at work told me that no one up north spoke Spanish.
        Is this true?
I only see smooth fields of white,
Expansive, endless, empty.
And the blizzards, how will they be?
        A torrent of chaos that locks you in and lets you watch it from
                the inside, as though you were part of a snow globe?
Living beneath a shaken glass world, safer than the hands that shake you.

        ¿No hay muchos Mejicanos en Wisconsin?
        Si, es la verdad.
Beto and Ociel have never heard of Wisconsin.
They repeat it awkwardly; there are too many strange English syllables in
        that word
            Wisconsin
It is no *Tejas.*
        It is no Texas, with its flat southern valley that falls into Mexico.
        There are no memories that begin with your birth and wash
            over you,
        Eternal summers that beat down on dead grass,
        Journeys south, dirty border towns, calls of *guerrita.*
White,
        White,
            Snow White,
                Ivory,
                Alabaster,
        Is this how it will be?
        Whiter than the make-believe heavens that await us?
        Or will it be brown like you?
            Brown like warmth, brown like the inside of a dream
            Brown like the roots of ash juniper and the flowers
                of a *huisachillo* tree
            Brown like tenderness, brown like the breath
                of your sleep
            Brown like the bottom of a garden and the top
                of a jasper gem.

        Yes, indeed, there is no telling what it will be.

Leah Chin Christian

Seguin

What did she
do in long summer
afternoons standing
inside the small
square window
three houses over
from our house? Her
son faint
and washed out
in my memory
except for stiff
blonde crew cut, a
small boy's
thin shoulders,
tanned elbows and knees.

Their house a white
wood shingle with no
front sidewalk. No
husband we knew of
in our church or
at the nearby grocery.
Somehow I heard
she was from Seguin.
A place I didn't
know, a place I
forever linked
with a thin woman's
tall shadow in a house
I never entered. The flat
plane of empty, the troubled
call for home. A
starched white blouse
behind a high screened window
over an empty kitchen sink.

SARAH CORTEZ

Lakeside, Lake Houston

Here, the flagrant moon.
Spangles of light
embellish nocturnal antics
on the water's brim.
A rush of blue cool,
then fireflies, fancy matings.
Softly, a riot of resonance.

                    Janis Butler Holm

Christmastide / the Texican Border

Mild, sheep weather,
star-harboring skies,
a traveler's moon;

stones to pile up,
sit upon, make a fence,
roll away from a tomb;

cicadas singing *glorias*,
flowering olives for prayer,
fig trees cursed and blessed;

Palma Christi for donkey feet,
for sparrow homes,
for Solomon's sweets;

the passion flower of cacti,
sand to write a message in,
posadas to journey in hope;

and a river, wide and deep,
where, crossing to either side,
we are baptized anew.

                    Jan Seale

The Trough, Barbarosa, Texas

The bulb-lit sign with the arrow
says *BEER*, a greeting extended
like a secret handshake. Inside,
shuffleboard sand and road dust
settle into cracks in conversation
while bottles come over the bar
in exchange for stories. Outside,
beyond the blanched picnic tables
and thirsty cotton fields, the sky
goes to orange and purple neon
as the sun comes sliding down
the long, dry throat of evening.

Michael Hill

Lake Travis

for Edi

The telephone answering machine
plays back her death. Aneurysm—
your daughter . . . thirty seven.
From a porch chair, I watch moon tracks
stretch across the lake like visible
thought, me to you. Cedars shrub
the shore, cast moon-edged shadows
over fossils and limestone. In '87

the lake was low, used up by farmers
and residents that dry, dry summer.
Clams big as a fist gave up their secrets,
died in the sun. Water went back
almost to old riverbanks exposing part
of a stone wall piled stone on stone.
Those rocks, stood out for weeks, led
the eye underwater to mysterious ends.

The lake is high today. Water presses
equally on each side of the now-invisible
fence, passes through, around and over it.
I like to think our souls, solid as stones,
lie one on another stacked high
like some celestial fence while night and day,
life and death, exerting equal pressure,
pass through and around and over us.

U. T. Abercrombie

Wile E. Coyote's Lament

A drop of a thousand feet
and the canyon becomes a coffin.
Nature's ability to swallow
everything whole gives it power.
Poised at the top,
I have exhausted memory
searching for a charitable way out.
All I feel are the best of times,
a simple loss of a thousand dreams
floating past on the back
of West Texas breezes.

I have hiked and died
a thousand times in this country.
All the things I thought missing
I found in simple flowers
braced against the wind,
bushes lodged in the lip of a cliff,
streams rubbing up against muddy banks.
But even here, among a solitude so forgiving,
something desperate calls,
and sometimes a drop
of a thousand feet seems like
only the next step forward.

Larry L. Fontenot

A Place Called Poetry

There is a place called Poetry
that snuggles in the countryside
of northeast Texas. A farm road
leads there, meandering past
fallow fields and a smattering
of small ranches to a cluster
of houses and a few old churches.

Nearby, the Dry Creek Cemetery
wraps its arms around early English,
Scottish, Irish, and Welsh pioneers.
A marker by the cemetery gate relates
the history of the town, which was
originally called Turner's Point.

Elisha Turner, who received
the land for service to the Republic
of Texas, probably never gave
a thought to the name others
called the place where he settled.
He had more important things
on his mind, most likely, such as
extracting sustenance from the land.

But when a name change was required,
it's a blessing that local merchant
Maston Ussery looked up from his
shelves and ledgers one spring day
and remarked how the view outside
reminded him of a poem. And Poetry
came to life that day, the way it does
when someone looks beyond the surface
of necessity into the depth of possibility.

Linda Banks

Fridays

From the sun's showy descent
oil slicks on the highway burn smoky pink.
I travel west from Houston
turn onto the gravel road
roll down the window
breathe deeply
drive slowly
past the line of darkening trees
the red, rusted shed
the field of golden coreopsis
and lavender thistle.

The sun on my left now and almost gone
I travel the rise of road
too late to see the longhorns
but in time for the two black horses
on the rim of the hill
shining blue against the last arc of day.

Here the road veers right.
If you look down the long gorge
you can see the buildings in Dime Box.
Following the curve of earth, I continue.
See how the trees are taking back
their shadows. A light wind ripples
the stillness. Inside the fence, someone
has stacked stones into three pyramids.
Cairns marking the setting sun, our path.
Listen, you can hear them—

This is where the road takes me.
This is what the wind tells me.
This is the hymn of the stones.

LAURA QUINN GUIDRY

Washington on the Brazos State Park

Located near Navasota, this is the site where the Texas Declaration of Independence from Mexico was written and signed. It is also an ancient crossing site over the Brazos River.

Drop back in time
drop back
beyond
declarations of independence
drop back
gathering pecans
as you move
down hill toward
the Brazos,
as you think of other
backs going back
way back
to when
only a path
led down to the bank
for crossing
as your hand bends down
to scoop
the fruit
out of the prickly park brush,
like a handshake
back through
centuries, fingers reaching,
touching across
time flowing like water,
back
ancestors bending and picking
back
       back

Chuck Taylor

Texas

Texas is a brand burned in the eye
of a longhorn steer,
needing water,
and not finding any.

Anthony Russell White

Moon over Mineral Wells

The moon shone orange over Mineral Wells
and highway traffic started to slow down.
Moon craters looked a bit like little bells.

When heaven beams brilliance the spirit swells;
as drivers honked and cheered this Texas town,
the moon shone orange over Mineral Wells.

This low sky pumpkin wove soft magic spells,
the moon's man smiled, then wink-laughed like a clown.
Moon craters looked a bit like little bells.

Can evil spaceships come in such bright shells,
a witch in fairy-gold godmother gown?
The moon shone orange over Mineral Wells.

Two nearby planets mimicked caramels,
and apple-bobbing thoughts reversed my frown.
Moon craters looked a bit like little bells.

While my poet's mind created villanelles,
autumn's sweet verb replaced summer's hot noun.
The moon shone orange over Mineral Wells.
Moon craters looked a bit like little bells.

J. Paul Holcomb

An East Texas Pond Speaks

In winter gray with white edges
I lie outside the hustle of town.
Once isolated, now I am encircled
by brick and glass, and children
skimming stones across my skin.
The children and I get along, but
bulldozers on empty lots make
me tremble, scaring the ducks,
ruffling their feathers as they paddle
into my broadest space.

A blue heron settles on shore,
scans my depths for a morsel,
takes a drink and lifts its wide wings
in quickened flight.
Two young deer passing by
nod once before running
as if the hounds of Baskerville
were at their tails.

The noise is unearthly.
Astronauts pass to another world,
and a burning piece of tile drops
from the sky into my lap.

SHIRLEY HILL

A Hymn for the River

Santa Elena Canyon, The Rio Grande

What the conquistadors felt
when they named this canyon
for the fierce and pious empress
mother of Constantine, I can only guess.
There's not a trace of holiness
here unless you find something sacred

in the liquid seam of river binding
nation to nation: Mexico's Chihuahua
a sheer cliff; Texas a pebbled bank
laced with green. And it's hot,

as only desert Texas can be hot.
We shuck our boots and wade
to the knee-deep center then plant
our heels to feel the current flow
between our legs. Indecent. Wonderful.

Stumbling ashore, we lie flat
on our backs so we can watch a raptor
ride a slim updraft of air, so high
I think I'm imagining him. But I don't
imagine the warmth of your hand on my hip.

I'm not alone though I feel
the loneliness of sandstone and ocotillo
like a singing along my spine.
So here's a hymn for the river
whose motion is silver. For canyon walls
that rise like the arms of a supplicant
in a place holier than its name.

CLAIRE KEYES

West Texas Permian Basin

Black
pump jacks
dot the western deserts;
stoic dinosaurs,
see-saws
in coyote country,
candelabra cacti
in fields of sage
at home in Western Texas.

YVONNE NUNN

Driving Across Texas in Winter

Grains of snow. Wind. A couple dozen black Angus
pressed together along one side of a collapsing barn
someone should have dismantled years ago.
A few miles on, an old blue Dodge up on blocks
in some family's yard where a rusting flatbed
piled high with rectangular hay bales
idles in the driveway. Far ahead nothing
but two-lane asphalt grayed by dust
and the fine, sandy gravel left after the last snow.
Miles later a yellow VW on the roadside, its hood up
like the promise of sunshine gone sour.
Hours of sky without a single bird in it.
Our favorite radio station crackles
and disappears. Hardly another car or truck
in either direction, then a dark speck
on the other side of the two-lane becomes
a man with his collar closed around his neck,
his head down, thumb out. At the wheel
my husband sighs. He used to hitchhike
highways like this in weather like this
when he was young and did what he pleased.
Before long we'll need fuel, restrooms,
a bag of chips or a chocolate bar. We'll need
the drawl of a convenience store worker
closing the drawer of the register
and saying without looking up,
"Y'all come back now, ya hear?"

Andrea Hollander Budy

Deserted Home Place

Weeds grow up over an abandoned van
parked in a field by Daddy's barn.
Dusty webs guard his house of plans,
where his tools rust like divorced dreams.

The creek chokes on watercress
where the willow wept gracefully
where the willow swept by the wind
lies fallen. Logs float in the lake.
The buildings about cry for repair
and the trees despair in the vines.
All just echoes of the past.
The gate is now padlocked fast.
Potholes without hope in red rock road
remind me how much we cared,
of the grooming we gave this land,
the toil and love we shared.
The house scarred by neglect
keeps the secrets had in its rooms
like a sad supply of lost hopes
in bastions made for an era's end.
The land will toast a new tenant
with clumps of daffodils,
their golden lips blowing
whispers, like real words
with the sweet scent of knowing
why we plant flowers in the dirt.

BETTY DAVIS

EAST TEXAS FLASHBACK

Now cottonwood leaves plane down—
small yellow fans the shape
of large paper ones we waved,
sitting through summer sermons
that spoke of a better place
than the metal chairs we sat on,
in the cement-floored church
with its narrow carpet runner
defining the central aisle,
down which you'd walk to be saved.

JEAN H. MARVIN

A Thousand Moons

I remember what was there:
Patterson's Grocery, the old man's filling station,
and the Ritz, its marquee long shattered even then.

When it was summer, we rocked on the porch.
Steam rose from gutters, and whenever we walked
we walked in the shade.

After supper we walked to the railroad tracks and back.
From every porch, radios stuttered farm reports, and at night
a thousand moons would burn upon a thousand windows.

Mama would lie on her sheetless bed, her foot tapping
against the bedstand. Then there were her muffled cries,
as her whisky breath mixed with the summer night's humidity.

Nothing I have is mine.
When I was a child
I thought the fields and ditches, even sounds—
Grandma driving her flat bed up the gravel drive,
and the wind pressing the loins of weeping willow
against my window—were mine and mine alone.
But that is not the way it is.

Ken Wheatcroft-Pardue

Drive Through

Texas Department of Highways
built a new exchange for I-30 and 820.
The ramp from 30 East to 820 South runs
through what used to be my bedroom in high school.
Thomas Wolfe was not completely correct.
You might not be able to go home again
but you can drive through it a couple of times a week.

Michelle Hartman

Visit to the Texas State Aquarium

Master of disguise
Now you see it, now you don't
Flounder in the sand

Junette Kirkham Woller

The River and the Man

He steps along the river hunting rocks,
aware the river's hunting him. He tries
to leave but can't. He's back again

to clamber over stones and silt
watching for the special something
that the river wants for him.

He thinks sometimes that certain pebbles
lugged to light and heaved into the car
will take him back to Llano once
he's safely home, far from the river,

but he forgets, of course, that the water's
infinite in patience. Though it seems
to change as it rushes to get somewhere,
it's really going nowhere except

into his heart where its granite blue
pounds red, and the green of wonder
in his childness reaches deep

and will not leave him anything
but restless, only restless, ever restless,
for a mighty dream of water, silt, and rock.

George Klawitter

Fishing the Frio River

Time is a meandering river.

It is this brook
I fish and swim,
upon which oar strokes measure hours
of the day.

I drink from it,
pull stubborn trout shiny as gold coins
from its swift and pebbly deep, its thin current sliding
always to the sea.

I stop rowing, listen
to the waterfalls, wishing

that I could live my life
as deliberately as a stream.

John E. Smelcer

Driving the U-Haul

I drove my parents' U-Haul from San Diego to Houston. A good opportunity to spend some time with them and lend them a hand. We drove four days and entered Houston's city limits late in the afternoon of the fourth day, in pouring rain and rush hour traffic. I couldn't help noticing that the overpasses, arcing above me like lasagna noodles, were incomplete.

No construction continued, but lanes were left hanging to be finished later, I suppose. And there were stacks of concrete obelisks as high as skyscrapers. The same barriers used to define HOV lanes and entrance ramps. Neatly criss-crossed, like Lincoln Logs left outside in the rain but expected to be played with later. The size of the cranes can only be imagined.

We drove past retention ponds, drainage ditches, slumps of mud retreating from overpass embankments. Bayous for flood control, though signs still give them names. Mountains of sand, gravel, dirt—urban resources, and concrete rubble—detritus and resource as high as buildings rising above the flood plain on which Houston is built.

Exits went off in either direction—get right to take Loop 610, get left for the North Freeway, across four lanes of bumper-to-bumper traffic. Seventeen miles from Katy to the Loop, around the Loop to Interstate 45, past suburb after suburb, mall after mall, exit after exit. Through it all, my father sat leaning forward in the seat next to me, watching for the sign of his exit.

"How much farther, Dad?"
"We should be there soon, Son."

BRADLEY EARLE HOGE

Big Bend Suite

Chihuahuan desert:
spring is a horseman fording
the Rio heading north.

The mountain lion
turns day and night to danger
high in the Chisos.

Santa Elena:
canyon carved by Rio Grande
to sheer granite walls.

From desert roadsides
cheering us with spring's promise:
Big Bend bluebonnets.

Spring sun awakens
slumbering yucca cacti—
flowerbursts of snow.

GLEN SORESTAD

A Rare but Passionate Ode to Houston

Maybe they hate you, Houston,
because they haven't lived you:
haven't lived those soft summer evenings when
brash crickets bray in their dark beds,
grasshoppers wait green with yearning or envy
and blue mosquito hawks hunt under the eaves.
Or maybe they've never lain at night
on a still-warm sidewalk or just
haven't stroked the breathing belly of a toad.
Could be they've never seen cicadas flap frantically
out and away from their capsular wombs
and heard the desperate joy of the cicada-song
they've waited seventeen years to sing.
Maybe they've never rolled with a lover
on fresh-mown St. Augustine grass,
haven't smelled wisteria in March,
haven't stood still in sudden surprise at
the relentless coming of a blue norther.
Or maybe they do know you, reckless place,
but can't bear what's wild in the world.

Mary G. Parham

Seeing the Marfa Lights

Small globes on the horizon
glowing as though with sunlight
pulsing, shivering as though in wind

here on the edge of the wide, black plain,
only a cold stillness pricked with a few stars,
a lopsided half-moon

and the older couple huddled in lawn chairs,
a pair of binoculars between them
as they tell us the story of the lights.

Look! There's one now—and another—
offering the binoculars to each of us in turn
as though it's crucial that we see

this mystery the Indians described
as stars come down to earth,
the way they bloom like rounded candle flames

sometimes divide in two, float up, sink down
blink out then reappear as suddenly
as they left as though to say

Wait! What you thought was gone
can reassemble itself once more,
shimmering on some dark, outstretched shore.

Patricia Spears Bigelow

the first time
i came
here, i was
sold. i knew
the clichés, of course;
but they turned
out to be
mirrors of
the truth.
the sky is
much larger than
the land we
live on. each day
the sky opens
and grants
permission to sit
on the roof
with my shirt off
drinking beer.

Michelle Paulsen

A Moment from the Dance

The Rifle Club Hall, Orange Grove, Texas, 1958

We danced past midnight, summer sweating us
like bourbon's smoky dare, Gulf breeze swirling
through dance hall windows, a whisper of salt
and sea to cool the evening heat, darken
into something like desire, its promise
of kisses languorous as slow dancing
against keen serenade of steel guitar.

We cooled ourselves outdoors beneath light bulbs
strung from post to post, bottle caps rippling
at our feet, scattered there like sand to crunch
beneath our dancing shoes while bartenders
dispensed us bottles wet with ice, tossed caps
upon the glinting record of our passing.

DAVID MEISCHEN

Slow Darkness over Houston

Brightness falls—
a phrase for Renaissance poets
and elegiac novelists
and other specialists in anguish

a phrase that does not belong
to the grounded grammar
of everyday Saturdays

where morning stars are wishes
and newspapers and theses
and a shuttle speeding home

brightness remaining in the sky
where we want it to belong.

PEGGY LIN DUTHIE

Driving West Texas

Cotton tufts cling to withered plants
in fields that stretch to the horizon.
"Have faith? Buy an umbrella!"
the hand-made sign proclaims
from the gas-station corner
in this time of spring drought.

On ranches here and there
the oil wells pump,
and the miles pass, a monotony
punctured only by mirage
and robotic dinosaurs
dipping into the earth,
sucking up the black death
of their ancestors.

Penny Harter

By the Guadalupe

A sycamore leaf set sail
on a river of glass,
riding buoyant powers
and the green sheen of summer
to a small conclusion
beyond observation.
I was timid to the touch of cold water,
barefoot on smooth boulders
amid the moorings
of giant cypress roots.
But the little boat floated,
immediate and beckoning,
around a bend
in the liquid corridor,
and for a moment
I was pleasure dancing on the rim of self.

Suzanne Freeman

Red Truck

Out in the country, where land
provides a living if a man works
at it—it's not there for the giving—
spring rains are enough to start

cotton, sorghum and other grains.
Cattle graze on thick grass or laze
in the shade of pin oak and pecan
trees. Out in the country, where trucks

feel at home and free to roam,
a '49 Chevy pickup moves along
the two-lane blacktop, slowly—
but it moves. Its original paint job

is faded but still red. The original
owner behind the wheel is faded
too. He raises two fingers as we pass.
I raise a friendly hand, chance

a glance at the mirror and see
only the empty road to forever.

JOHN E. RICE

Pure Cane Syrup

All spring and summer, and well into October, they are there,
on the roadsides of East Texas—clumps of enterprise—
pickup trucks, tailgates lowered toward the traffic,
piled with produce (home-grown, red-ripe, fresh-picked).
The producer sits in a folding chair under the pine shade
watching the mobile flow, hoping for a stop, a howdy, a sale,
making change from his cigar box or a sugar sack.
He has set his trap well—for half a mile his amateur signs
announce at hundred-yard intervals his tempting delights.

124

Mayhaw jelly. Tomatoes. Fresh-picked corn. Shelled peas.
Yard eggs. Sweet potatoes. Honey. Pure cane syrup.

Some days he does pretty well—city folks in new cars
are reminded of their country past, their small town roots,
and stop to buy a nostalgic taste of the good old days:
two pounds of hand-shelled purple hulls, green onions,
a few vine-ripened tomatoes, red as a fireplug.
She asks the Fates who control club meetings, bridge parties,
and mall walks when she will ever find time to cook them.

Vendors who have done well often build open-air stands,
semi-permanent displays for home-grown peaches, watermelons.
And a few larger places offer pungent-smelling Bar-B-Q.
There are big-rig truckers who will bring a load of logs
to a whistling air-brake stop for that.

If you want to check on the produce business in East Texas,
you will have to drive state roads and through little towns.
There are no big smiles, no sweat to mop, or stories to swap
on the sterile and seamless Interstate.

JAMES O. DOBBS

DRIVING HOME AT NIGHT THROUGH THE HILL COUNTRY

I felt the hills enfold me
gentle with time
the trees breathing on me in the darkness.
This is how
a man should come home—
to the right earth:
not to labor on it
but to be known;
not to stand on it
but to lie full length
remembering with his whole weight.
Memory is a thing of bone.

ALBERT HUFFSTICKLER

Lullaby for a Tiny Texas Town

with loving memories of Mullin, Texas, hometown of my
maternal grandparents, Mr. & Mrs. H.T. Deaver

In Ivy's store, a dusty window pane
Proclaims a cruel message: "Mullin's dead!"
What thoughtless scribe traced in the dust this bane
That swells my throat with ache of tears unshed?

The tiny town's not dead, just slumbering,
Absorbed in pleasant dreams of yesterday—
Of butter churns and creaking front porch swings,
And life before the young folks moved away.

Farmhouses weathered silver by the sun,
Hold memories too dear to count as dead—
When whittling and dominos were fun,
And luxury was grandma's feather bed.

An ancient windmill croons a lullaby,
While Mullin drowses 'neath a Texas sky.

VALERIE MARTIN BAILEY

Field Hospital, 1876-1891, Fort Davis, Texas

No more voices barking out orders
No more hooves dancing on the desert rubble
No more swords sharply slicing the wind
Only the wind rattling tin caissons on the roof
Only a raspy wren running its next meal through
on the dagger of its beak

No more beds
No more gunshot or arrow wounds
No more gangrene field amputations
No more cries

No more iodine carbolic acid
No more quinine or mercury pills
No more cries

No more fevers
No more cold cloths at the temples
No more soothing hands speaking of home
No more heroes no more malingerers
No more cries

Only a shell of a building
speaking through crumbling bricks
decrepit drafty halls
speaking our whole story in silence
Only a shell of a body
entrusted to our small ephemeral hands
and to the grinding mouth of the canyon wind

MARCELLE H. KASPROWICZ

HUECO TANKS

we wish for
mouse bones
joints that collapse & shift
slip like smoke
through webbed fissures
that mar
this rocky thunderhead
basins & hollows store
precious water in arid land
petroglyphs
& other graffiti
   john holden 1849
   brandon ♥ chantal
i resist the urge
to mark my passage

ANN HOWELLS

Chisos Mountains at Twilight

The palette is
red, yellow, blue and purple,
the subject, ghosts.
Sky turns to shale,
as colors streak the slopes
north of the Big Bend.
Petroglyphs, dugouts, caves
leave with the day.
Details are now phantoms
flitting from rock to rock,
cliff to crevice,
breaching the twilight boundary
between worlds.
The Chisos rids itself
of all that has no business here.
It is all haunting.
No longer mountains
but the outline of fear
against night.

John Grey

Road in the Thicket

Vultures soar overhead, curse circles in the haze,
crowd out the ragged crows at the road-kill,
a bloody feast of matted rabbit meat or coon,
armadillo laid flat on this asphalt plate
for dark scavengers to commune and partake.
Muscadine vines weave with poison ivy,
twist and twine in spring with yellow jessamine
bells that dangle high in long-leafed pine.
Chalky bare branches of sycamore and ash
tower above passing cars, tractors and trucks.
Meandering sloughs creep through the thicket,
slip into culverts under black tar roads,
flood grassy ditches where snakes and crawfish grow

deep in the mud hiding from the makeshift signs
of the others—the folk—selling lumber, quilts, bird-
houses, and sweet honey; selling junk, some trinkets—
stuff bartered and sold for life along the road,
past the vultures picking bones clean,
past poison flowers dangling high.

CAROLYN TOURNEY FLOREK

Nomadic Blunder

Texas, I left you for four years,
had my eyes on every other state
with more than two syllables
and easily found one willing to play
house. I brought little of you
with me—hoping to forget, wanting
to break in a new state of mind
like a squeaky new pair of shoes,
but soon found the skin
of my Achilles' heel rubbed raw.

Where else can one turn for gauze
when the injury is Texas-sized?
When the homesickness is more than
an aching sternum that is rash-red
from stroking knuckles attempting
to apply pressure to a weeping wound?
Or more than a vacant hunger just behind
the belly button that somehow tugs
relentlessly at the milky membrane
that surrounds your memory?

I sped down I-35 and didn't relax the grip
on my helm until I sailed past Town
Lake. The scar finally forming
when I entered Bexar county—I came home.

LORENA FLORES-KNIGHT

Someday When I Am an Old Woman and My Heart Is a Movie Theatre of Memories, Let Me Replay This One

You never know when happiness might rise:
an outburst of quiet fire catching beneath
your skin. Sometimes all it takes is a town
called Comfort, a small park with a white
gazebo and a circular path around it just
right for the children to ride their bikes.

It is almost spring, a bit breezy but warm
enough: knots of green glimmer high
in certain trees, three stone churches stand
nearly side-by-side, launch pad of a long white
see-saw with all four of us finally astride—
everything comes together and we ride the rise of it.

Each moment flows from the fingers
of the one before it, a creek of soft joy,
the children pedal down church lane
and remember to slow at the intersection
and look, sun glints off the helmets.
Your husband easy in the unexpected drive,

the uncertainty of where we might find a place
to ride off these unknown byways. Then there
it is—gazebo and shy steeples. You park,
lift the latch on the station wagon,
sunlight tender upon exposed arms,
blue sky unstoppable above you.

Cyra S. Dumitru

The Ride

In the front seat of our Biscayne,
on a night ride home from the country
with my father,
cold spring air poured in the window—

welcome, like cool sheets in a summer bed.
The passing musk of some wild animal
faded into the dusk,
lights from a distant town
sparkled on the horizon
as if on the edge of a black table.
The air was rich with the scent
of wet earth and field grass.
In that quiet hour,
we savored the drone of tires
on county pavement,
as we memorized the calls of birds
from the dark prairie.
We measured the breadth
of the sky
from star to star,
relishing the fullness of eternity
in that single moment,
that one night
before the end of the world.

Carolyn Adams

Texas

I unfold to the breadth of sky,
inhale bluebonnet and sage,
flatten my spine to this ground,
feel a tilt of stomach at the race
of clouds felling the loft of cities
and country apples too-early green.

Through the press of storm, I hold
on to both the thrust of planes
and the pulse of hooves,
and I laugh that I ever dreamt
of herding sheep in Wyoming.

Sandra Gail Teichmann

At The Pedernales River Gorge

Through peeling cypress an imagined path,
scattered with juniper berries,
descends like insistent hope
to a layered limestone jumble, the river bed.
The water's low. You plant yourself
on a rock, meander on the golden underwing
of an airborne hawk.
Someone skips a stone—
blue diamonds flash where the river widens
drawing your glance to cross
and climb a vertical face, cratered as an old man's.
Higher up you can see through an eye
to blue on the opposite side—
here below, the wind-hollowed cheeks
are rich in odd encounters
where seeds that spiraled down
took hardy root and grew
a whisker of oak or aspiring shrub
the way we all fill niches in other people's lives.

Nancy Kenney Connolly

This Place

The river runs through
This place, this place
That I call home.
It rises each day through
The mesa, lifting slowly,
Burning white.

Here all things turn white,
Even the poppy blooms
Blood drained in this
Place where the earth
Crackles and the bedrock
Lies exposed.

It's my place of dirty
Old stones, a place that stays
Land dusty and crusted with fossils.
Roots and bones litter the forest,
All bleached by the scorch of
A white-hot muse.

Her amnion presides
Over this place, my garden.
I feel it raw, baring all of its edges,
And smelling dank
Like a full-bodied mother
Primed only to protect,
Or kill.

JOY PALMER

THE STORE AT WINCHELL, WATERCOLOR

All those mornings as my car
swept past the highway's bend,
the old store caught the blast of sunrise,
flashed it back. Again, again.

I, triumphant driver of the days,
thought to keep that light.
"Mary," I said, "you must paint that scene,
catch the light for me."

And now I have your painting, a good-bye gift
when I left behind the prairie sun,
its harsh hopefulness, the light's lift. And though
water's sadness runs through the scene,

still I have this blessing drawn from old walls,
from the curve, from the moving on.

MARGIE McCRELESS ROE

Homesteading

He drove her up a puckered path
Cut clean between the cleavage
Of the cedared cliffs
And scrub brush climbs
Until they disappeared
Into the canyon cut
With shadows chasing close behind

Then he did to her
What he had done
With all this cactus
Sand and stone
He put a fence
Around her heart
And called her love
His own

Anne McCrady

Two Hours to Write a Poem

My hat is missing, the old straw one,
greasy around the band. It would hold
in the words I want, keep out the plague

of thoughts, like gnats waiting for an
open-scalp lunch: *Do the bills, write
sympathy notes, file papers.* My index

fingers hold the rise on the F key and
the J key, prepare to launch a poem.
Wonder World. The road to Wimberley

filled with eye-splintering turquoise and red
signs, *It's Texas' Fault, Experience
Texas Caverns, Turn at Exit 202,*

should work. Imagine the height, the pure
stalactites, stalagmites, the cascade of water
surging from the underground spring,

the waterfall of Mystery Mountain falling
over limestone rocks into sweet Texas air.
Ditch the beer image. Imagine my

hat firmly in place on my head,
imagine we spotted the turn-off sign
and actually visited Wonder World Park.

U. T. ABERCROMBIE

TEJANO COUNTRY

The radio speaks in English,
but it sings in Spanish.

The cotton fields are bilingual
and full of unconsummated love.

The combine driver whistles
romance to his plain-faced girlfriend.

Tribal accountants prepare for another
profitable winter at the Inn of the Mountain Gods.

(My only objection is my failure
to spot even one armadillo.)

I've just crossed into New Mexico.
I will carry Texas home with me

with the gleam of a hawk's eye
and a tornado in my heart.

MEL C. THOMPSON

THE PELICAN NOTES

two oceans
of brazoria
county

side by side

separated
by a thin strip
of quintana beach

to the east
the larger
sea-green
gulf of mexico

to the west
the smaller
red sea
of indian blankets

CAROLYN LUKE REDING

Time Is Linear

I park outside the Petroleum Club,
and the building doesn't recognize me.
The courthouse on Belknap, caked in layers
of cosmetic surgery, nods a stoic hello.

In Abilene, Uncle Walter's old Barcalounger remembers me,
but it's never warm now when I sit in it.
And Aunt Ruth's Fina station died when they dug up its leaking tanks;
its windows dark and staring, its open door a black *Oh!* of surprise.

Walter's old farm truck sleeps now against a mesquite in the side yard
where rocks long ago took the sight from its rusting headlamps.
Still, when I haul up onto the wooden bed, it wakes to my touch
and remembers when I was just a boy.

It remembers carrying us through newly planted fields at night
as we shot jackrabbits from its broad back under the burnished glare
of those once bright eyes. It remembers our laughter as we bounced,
like watch springs, while it lunged over the furrows.

In Big Spring, the old outdoor arena still echoes the sounds of rodeo,
but the cement powder of its bleachers no longer bounds away
dancing like twin, beckoning moons on the blue-jeaned bottoms
of young West Texas girls.

Slowly, it seems, the proofs of my past are being replaced
by the future memories of a new layer of lifetimes,
and only now, as my heart moans like a cello,
am I beginning to believe it is even possible to grow old.

JOHN BROOKS

Local Music

Take Texas—
hawked, hyped, clichéd, inflated
to an enormous abstraction.
Refined, distilled down
to a simple sound,
its essence is concentrated
into a few clear notes:
some lonely ranch hand's wife
soothing her simpering child
with a song sung sweet and low,
echoed by the soprano squeal
of a windmill's wheel which becomes
the wail of the wind slipping through
barbed wire strands—the true
High Plains Drifter, wild and free,
headed for the coast
and the open sea.

JOHN E. RICE

I'm an Old Man

Do the gods congregate
at the Barton Springs
of heaven? Do they
come in T-shirts and
shorts with dogs looping
the grass? Do flies buzz
the picnic tables where
the gods set out
their wine and cheese?
Do the gods rent canoes?
Do they wait in line
to purchase tickets
to take their children
for rides on a miniature
train? How long can
a god hold his breath,
breast-stroking beneath
cold spring waters?
Will the turtles come
and nibble a god's toes?
I'm an old man.
I want to know.

CHUCK TAYLOR

Texas Journey

Outsiders know of our big land,
joke of day-long trips
without a border-dent.

But straight up, if some cartographer
could demarcate, the state
holds equal sky-territory.

They sing of stars shining bright
and yellow roses and ten-gallon hats.

But listen closely to the distance
and the wind and the road-silence.

It's true. You can drive
all day and never
reach the end

but didn't Ulysses call
for such horizons? What hero
would not want vast Texas spaces?

Go west young man.
Just a phrase, just words today,
unless the trip is in this state
still worthy
of lone stars
and land voyages.

ADAM BERLIN

MORNING WALK

The pungent fragrance of cooking jalapeños
Comes on an easterly breeze
With a puckered mouth
As I step onto the street again.
A displaced Leghorn rooster
Cracks the dawn on
Lincoln Street
Answered by a horned owl
Perched, waiting for breakfast
On the heights above Woerner Warehouse.
It's not the breeze that raises
Goose bumps on my forearms
But the wordless wonder
The encompassing grace
The Sanctus bells of an ordinary morning.

JACK SWANZY

Davis Mountains

Texas sunset lingers
as my plane moves west
saving hours by the minute
to forestall the time
I will break into song
eulogy for the sun's
heated vistas worlds apart
from topside running rivers
lakes flowing into black holes
collages of villages and towns.

With steady foothold
on glacier-sturdy clouds
the sun does not die
and if I painted this
you would say
it could not be real:

scarlet strokes above
carrot orange casting out
to opaque sea-foam green
neon saffron bits
and psychedelic apple slices
cut by purple knife clouds
chocolate dripping into silver
light green again and then
cerulean blue to hug the moon.

Now I know
I have seen God.

Rouge and cardamom God.

One-hundred-percent
Red Hot God.

                    Martha Everhart Braniff

Vanishing over the Horizon

I believe in Texas   as a state of mind

the wide deserts   room for elbows

        and other desires—

cowboys

lonely and rambunctious   roping steer

           repairing fences

     then galloping wild

         over

           every   post.

Kicking up heels   the tap of boots

        a mantra

there is space in my life for the unexpected to occur.

I close the magazine

   saddle up my inner horse

     and ride into the orange sun

      vanishing

        over the horizon

         like a buffalo

          into the glimmering fields.

Dane Cervine

Night Passage

I step out on the porch,
coffee cup in one hand,
the other on the screen door as it closes—
I want to sit alone to watch the night end.

Distant lights across the bay
reflect orange on the glass-flat surface
and I see dim running lights of shrimp boats
moving slowly in the dark.

Gradually I make out channel markers
winking green and red,
those silent pairs that mark safe passage
in to port and out again to sea.

My mind drifts back
and I recall sailing home at night,
ghosting silently in the channel
between those pairs of welcome lights.

Now I can see low purple clouds
in the eastern sky—
I have savored the night's passing
and my day is well begun.

Jean Donaldson Mahavier

A Map of Texas

Dallas is allotted no more ink
than any other city, but my childhood
was drawn inside that spot, moving
vans drove its thin ink streets, and death
scrawled its signature in narrow alleys
that never made it onto maps. I can
buy a map of only Dallas, all its streets,

and still could not convey how big it is—
how even from a dot across the country,
it's so much harder to erase than this
small circle. It's the place I widened,
crawling out my window—direction,
destination, left in my room
next to schoolbooks. I set out to stretch
that dot to eruption. I never could
reach the edges. But that didn't keep me
in my room, even when my mother's
sleeping breath floated down the hall
and up the sidewalk behind me, to whatever
car I thought might drive me to the farthest
corners of that ink spot that I cover, now,
with one fingertip.

DEBORAH ROSSEL

EMPTINESS

Alone in the middle of a pasture
burned by summer heat,
my grandfather's house is forlorn and sad.
Broken windowpanes speak of neglect
and rock-throwing passers-by.
Crumbling roof gables and rotting porch pillars
give away its years.
Standing at the barbed wire fence a hundred yards away,
I try to imagine the time when six children,
born here to Emma and Joe,
filled its rooms with love and laughter and tears.
Long ago deserted by family
when the lure of jobs and love took them away,
the weathered house stands as if waiting for their return.

I am suddenly aware it has survived them all.

CAROL J. RHODES

Galveston in October

The sea is German silver here
A molten mass that never cools
Heavy metal singing
In a cauldron. Nothing ever stops.
      A hundred palms along the Seawall
      Dance like Fred Astaire and Ginger Rogers
      Green fronds waltzing cheek-to-cheek
      Against a backdrop of gray silk.
Choruses of sea-oats
Beach plum, kelp
Roll in, roll out
All day, all night.

And by the bay a square-rigged barque
Sways at her pier, masthead tilting
In the wind like some lost woman
Looking for a permanent address.
      Sand shifts each second, drifts through thoughts
      And pastel rooms. Even antebellum dowagers
      Rock slowly with the waves, outlasting war
      And storms, columns elegant, secure.
Nothing drowns this point and counterpoint
Bubbling in old pewter
Churning toward those closing chords
The ocean never plays.

Carol Coffee Reposa

Passenger Station, Texas

It keeps its memories of Texas swing,
excited children on their way to far-off
Dallas, trainloads of soldiers leaving home
or coming back at the end of World War II.
Forlorn, its windows vibrate only to
the passing freights; its rooms lie empty
save for now and then a boy or two
      entering on some dare.

Never having seen a huge black engine
full of noise and heat and steam
that made more timid kids run back
to their fathers' sides, they have no
frame of reference to make the place
more than just some dusty wooden
furnishings or secret haunt of creatures
          of the night.
But then, imagination has a way
of making history seem real.
So on a quiet day, if you listen carefully,
you'll hear the engine up the track,
and if you watch with eyes that still believe
you'll see the train come lumbering past,
filled with people smiling wide. They're
going home, you know, while the rest
of us will have to wait awhile
there beside the track, shaded by
the station at the city's downtown edge.

RALPH HAUSSER

Sutton County, Texas

Here is a land so harshly grandiose
it needs no anger to control goats,
sheep, deer, cacti and mesquite,
or men who choose to remain.
This place speaks quietly of fighting
a million wars interlocking,
disallowing disobedience with its
persistent way of resisting defiance.
By its own rules, survival of
its vested violence is assured,
the trust affirmed in whole worship,
offering adjacent fruit and thorns.
God must have loved giving
this grand space its own command.

BETTY DAVIS

Old Western Traces

Obscured, forsaken
obliterated in places
old roads endure
beyond generations
who never rode
their spaces.

Peggy Zuleika Lynch

St. Joe Island

Someone must praise small waves
that whisper up to beaches.
The constancy, the constancy!
Can anything be more steadfast
than small, determined waves?

The Texas sun loves chasing them till
just before they flatten quietly,
blending with the sand,
erasing Sarah's footprints, as they flow.

Sarah loves small waves;
they don't knock down her sand towns,
or at least not all the way.

And pipers find their tiny breakfast shellfish,
supper plankton, here
between the gentle rush and ebb.

On the Texas Gulf, a long way from the "Big Port"
but just above "Christ's Body," Corpus Christi,
is this island, left almost alone—
St. Joe, a stretch of Texas pure—
a curlew playground, and a gentle mother-sea
for lovers of small waves.

Joan Seifert

The Power of Stone

If you live in Texas Hill Country,
you must understand the power of stone.
Stone plaits the portrait of the land,
colors your waking, paints your dying.
You have to see the thrust of jagged teeth
into the sky, see it sewn into the earth,
into great escarpments rough-shouldering valleys.

You have to see it weaving arms of water into braided silver,
see it webbing streams, giving frames to lakes.
You have to see it stone-walling for miles,
snaking through fields, ruffling hills
like pumiced luster of satin or emery rub of tweed.

You must think of warp and woof, of granite deep in earth
holding reservoirs of life-giving water,
see stone wreathing cottages, courts, state houses.
Stone is the sturdy seed our seed met,
forming barriers to plains, lacing rims of coastal savannas.

When you leave, you dream of stone,
still listen for its voice.
It is essential
to imagine woven fabric of stone is still underfoot.

SHIRLEY JONES HANDLEY

Prayer for West Texas

Like the first exposure to Zen
the seductiveness of the place
wholly rests
in our contemplation of an infinite
nothingness.

Let's keep it this way.

PETER FOGO

Reading a Map

A segment in the corner reveals
an open field scattered with wild flowers
and the cadence of a galloping horse.

Look down a faint trail to find
the girlchild on horseback
at the moment she knows: *the soul means me.*

At the far end of the map
an old woman in dusty shoes
holds in her mind a place further back—

before the open field—to the fledgling
collecting acorns, humming
a single sound.

Katrinka Moore

Talk of the Towns: A Tribute to Texas Cities and Counties

The BISHOP gave his BLESSING, but Ana NEEDMORE.
Marriage to her was no EDEN on EARTH.

Her GROOM was a HUMBLE FARMER, not a RISING STAR,
more of a LONE STAR. His adventures in COMMERCE were NADA—
he barely had a DIME BOX, much less an OLD DIME BOX.

With no CASH, not even for a MULESHOE,
Ana was not HAPPY. She wanted her INDEPENDENCE,
to be FREER. She craved LIBERTY, LOVING COMFORT,
some GASOLINE, a CHINA set, a NEW HOME, a NEWCASTLE,
and no more of this DEADWOOD she was married to.

One FRIDAY at SUNDOWN, the GRIT began to GROW. They FAUGHT.
LEDBETTER! KRUM! TURKEY! BROADDUS!
BREWSTER! WISE GUY! DING DONG! FAIRY! CROW!
HALFWAY through Ana raised her middle finger and shouted, *UPSHUR!*

Then shouted, *WELCOME to DAINGERFIELD!*
and SWIFT, ANAHUAC'd him one with a SPADE,
CROSS CUT his face. The SHARP POINT PIERCE'd his skin.
She would have CUT AND SHOOT him, too, laid him out FLAT,
but GUN BARREL CITY NIX'd selling her a gun.
A good SHINER spread across the CENTER of his TEMPLE
as he SLIDE down the CONCRETE WALL.
Preferring DEEPWATER, Ana dug SEAGRAVES in the CISTERN
and SCURRY'd off into the ORANGE SUNSET with a SUBLIME HIGH,
which lasted until the police TELL her TWIN SISTERS.
Then it was CHAMBERS for her.

CHARLOTTE JONES

WHAT LAND

What land is this
that stretches like
a waking cat, and
turns its soil from
black to red to tan?
Who owns the hot
and endless desert's sand, the green pine forest thrusting
from the land? What magic spills the water to the shore of
beaches glowing with a perfect sun? It is a pinnacle of all
that earth can be, the best of tree and sky, the breathless
hush of sunsets on the plains. Our history is written in the stone that held the habitation
of native peoples, the blue horizon charting the carve of canyon—the heave of rock
as mountains grew from fault. And rivers mark our borders, cleave the ground
and rush with names like Red, Sabine, and Grande, to push past cities
rising from the fields of paintbrush, grass, mesquite. I know this state
shrine and monument that celebrate its future and its past. The
Alamo,   the Palo Duro Canyon, the places that
I   will cherish if I live a year or eighty in
its spell. What is this land that
knew my face and called
as if its bones had
always known
the language
of my name?

BUDD POWELL MAHAN

Lift-off from DFW Just after Dark

Streets and freeways, streams of light,
illumined arteries of traffic, clogged and trickling.
Holes in the galaxy below where lakes
are filling themselves with darkness,
poured from the sky into which
we glide. A cosmos of buildings
boxed in lighted outline, green and gold,
dense in the center and growing
smaller as we gain altitude
and finally tilt away.

Meanwhile beside me,
bathed in dome light, some passenger reads—
book-jacket illustration
of Marine emblems
and the title: *Close Combat*—
story told since Homer:
glory, mutilation,
making little of this miracle
of thirty planes held all at once in the same air.
Amber wing lights eerie on the rivets.

One meditates
on some star, it may be,
of self,
out of which we have dreamed
constellations
and then made them—
imagined ourselves birds
and became them.

Chris Ellery

IV. Logic of the Air:
Texas Weather & Seasons

Riding the Rain

It seems that we ride in the Ark
the way waves of rain pelt the sides
of our high home, the way water surges
from the deep, swirls above the threshold,
presses against windows which have yet to break.

Everything blurs. Days are the color
of a stone cracked open and night
that same stone overshadowed.
Green belongs to someone else's memory.
When was it that the last branch of the tallest

tree on our hill slipped beneath water,
when our stone home surrendered the foundation
and we began rolling from side to side? Cats hiss
from the windowsills, ceiling fans spin from the tumble
of it all. Stray rattlesnakes curl among

the cushions of our damp couches. I have
been named captain—my husband never learned
to swim. Our children stir potions to cure
seasickness, coming as we do from drought-stricken land.
The despair of what falls and rises without relent.

There must be a wisdom of waves,
but right now it is drowned out by the ceaseless
sound—the clicking clicking upon the roof.
Slap against storm windows which continue
to hold far beyond hope. Oh, for a plump

minute of silence. Glimpse of light. An even keel.

Cyra S. Dumitru

Clear Night, After a September Storm

To learn from fall, we should be alone.
Hear its breath on a sudden wind.
In its first chill sway, we are turned away

from sun. We cool with a worry
that colors have tricked us, summer

was nothing but a stream fed on flood,
deepened. We could accept leaving,
then, calmed by quiet, the surrender of

moments to distance. Had we forgotten
how stars, pulled free of sky at last,

would be loosed from the canvas of
what was? The wind moves like words
when one is a page for its silence,

and ready: to be written in yellow leaves,
to be settled by the logic of the air.

Steve Wilson

Apparition on Nueces Street

Austin, January 1973

Afternoon rain turned sleet, bitter
cold sweeping in from the Panhandle.
Streets froze like rippled glass and snow
powdered the ice. I stepped into winter night,
a dreamscape whispering white beneath moontower glow,
and a vision glided into the light, a skinny slouching Jesus in jeans,
hands in his pockets, vaguely smiling, gaze fixed on hereafter,
iceskates slicing into the night's white silence.

David Meischen

Texas Summer

Admit the sun is relentless. Birds ladle the sky—
every scalding blue inch of it—wing by wing
into your open mouth. Water is a luxury
only clouds can afford, but they're vacationing
over the Pacific. Grass screams from its earthen bed.
Admit: nothing you ever do is good enough.
The mosquitoes are calling your name.

Robert Wynne

Aftermath

A dark and dirty night is
backed into a corner by early
morning light. A red sun

scissors its way through
ragged remnants of clouds,
tries to find its way across

what used to be the Bay. The
Gulf backs away from gold
washed riprap, opening its

fine silk curtain revealing a
fresh swept beach. Prodigal
sandpipers wheel on wingtips,

touch down to hurry after our
fresh footprints tracking toward
whatever treasure glints in the

infinity ahead. Think how many
storms have we survived.

John E. Rice

Daybreak in a Time of Drouth

A slight transient freshness washes
the back lawn and the deck.
But still it's July and humid.
The stray cat I've fed for weeks
crouches and spits when I show up
and disappears through the fence.
It has not rained, will not rain.
The morning clouds burn by mid-morning
to a hot blue eye.
Will the cat forgive my humanness?
Will I succeed with the bougainvillea, letting it dry
to the point of death, they say, to force it to bloom?—
surely a sort of thought and motive
in the plant—how else to term it?—
it thinks of its death
and the last chance it has for blooming.

Mary Ellen Branan

Vegetable Love in Texas

Farmers say
There are two things
Money can't buy:
Love and homegrown tomatoes.

I pick them carefully.
They glow in my hands, shimmer
Beneath their patina of warm dust
Like talismen.

Perhaps they are.
Summer here is a crucible
That melts us down
Each day,

The sky a sheet of metal
Baking cars, houses, streets.
Out in the country
Water-starved maize

Shrivels into artifacts.
A desiccated cache
Of shredded life.
Farmers study archeology

In limp straw hats.
But still I have
This feeble harvest,
Serendipity in red:

Red like a favorite dress,
Warm like a dance,
Lush like a kiss long desired,
Firm like a vow, the hope of rain.

CAROL COFFEE REPOSA

Hunker Down

she said in the middle of a sentence
telling me about the time she
ran from the twister
and I thought
what an odd expression

but that's what she did
in a ditch
in a field
outside a small town
springtime in Texas
where some things remain wild and woolly

REBECCA HATCHER TRAVIS

Blue Norther

You can feel it in the air,
a blue norther is coming
to stir things up.
It blows across Texas
so cold you can see it,
whipping everything in its path,
knifing all that it touches.

I watch through my window
as freezing wind tears leaves
from branches that grab for me
like gnarled clawed fingers.
Sleet pellets hammer the walls
and rebound against my pane
like marble smashing marble.

The sly fox prowls around my house,
searching and lapping at each crevice,
but safe and warm inside I wait
until it decides to let me be
and move on to a weaker foe.

Jackie Pelham

Promise

On the grayest day
in winter, when even wet boots
would be better than the best
news you have heard lately,
and you need to clear the table
of your latest temptations
to be some place else,
take out a clean canvas.
Spill the milk of cirrus silk
across a spring-starched sky.

Draw an arrow, a piney line
pointing the way to heaven.
Give it limbs for fletching.
Fill the foreground
with the wild abandon
of azalea blossoms, honeysuckle
trumpets, redbud beads.
Add doe print, coon track,
webs of finest spider weave.
Count the miracles behind you;
consider the ones to come.
Recite the earthy promise
of the buckeye in your pocket:
another April in East Texas
is more than any man's fair share
of grace or good luck.

Anne McCrady

Midday, Midsummer

All morning the wind
blew rain out of the black
trees now a weave of sun
waves across a wall
of nandina vanishing
like a ball it's so bright
cicadas start winding up
their missionary pitch
a quick overcast and the
eyes have it a welcome
shade by the pool side
into the shadow of which
the shadow of a tiger
swallowtail lurches
giantly light as a bat.

Kurt Heinzelman

The Morning Porch

for Don and Lynn Watt

We stumble though an upswept hairdo of morning song—
grackles whoop and clatter like broken ceramics
frothed by runoff spinning through a culvert
while the golden nape of a woodpecker soft-strokes the live oak
on its rollercoaster flap to the waterfall.
Legions of white-winged doves ask their singular
                    who oh who who who
to the socked-in pantheist sky.

Fog-beguiled illiterates overwhelmed by the half-recalled
paragraphs of half-dreams, we speak in whispers
as if too much laughter this early might shatter the expanding universe,
our impossible need for clarity
to decode our own forgotten Rosetta stones.
Stunned as any clobbered frog by our hard rebirths
and blurred inside our shapeless desire,
we are so dumb with loneliness
we cannot really speak for wings we only guess.

Love is in the coffee steam,
sharing cream and the indecipherable chittering of squirrels
before fog banks shrink to reveal the all too real sweating sun.
Oh, this heavy San Antonio air is raw gray silk
that disguises each of us and our hunger
for bowls of fruit, their sticky pools of mingled juice,
the sweet grit of morning muffins.

What is art, but these fog-bound mornings
when we stagger from solitary sleep, learning
to bank the way a flock of swallows turns
all at once to feast on mosquitoes,
scruffy feathers synchronized to a single reflective wing?

PAMELA USCHUK

160

Island Ladies

When stormy winds blow inland
with great gusts of gods-gone-mad,
the cottages of Galveston
just seem to raise their latticed skirts
like the grand old ladies that they are,
accepting salt-soaked feet and flaking paint
with practiced grace.

These islanders have held their own
against rapacious forces,
learning how to bend not break,
to cope with change,
to age with fading charm.
Pretty they are not nor young,
but strong of beam with solid longleaf hearts,
they struggle with gentility
and pray for soft, sweet currents in the Gulf.

Joyce Pounds Hardy

Click

The birthday party day unexpectedly holds
a funeral too, Dutch chocolate torte layered
with *His Eye is on the Sparrow*.
Buddhist wedding ceremony, same day
H and P decide to split.
Comfort's General Store burns down
right before our neighbor's house is robbed.
One million acres of the Texas Panhandle
flaming, ten thousand animals
scorched. Three people told me
poetry saved their lives, on the same day they told me
this.

Naomi Shihab Nye

The Devil in East Texas

The Devil comes to East Texas
every summer—
when the folks step out
beneath his sky-high incubator,
the Bible Belt is loosened
and the britches of salvation
come sliding down—
down,
to the hot hot ground.

Chris McMillon

Wilshire Woods

Dragonfly summer comes to an end;
temperatures at last are tolerable.
Pecans tumble onto the roof,
intermittent as the ping
of beetles at the screen.
Too dazed with autumn to scamper,
front porch geckos hug the bricks.
Sycamore leaves in windswept swirls
settle in heaps by the fence.
There's nowhere else to go.

We will walk tonight
in the full moon's sheen
past alleys and post oaks,
down dark city streets
skittish with faded foliage.
The scene is familiar.
Your hand brushes mine,
your eyes dance colors.
We revel in a cool simmer
like insects off in the distance.

Scott Wiggerman

162

Winter Field, South Texas

All summer it waited for rain,
and now it waits for nothing,
black stumps of corn, what's left
of the crop after the drought.
What good can come
from this December sky,
heavy as a gun?

But then the clouds turn loose
the geese, thousands of them, until
the field swirls
in their churning blizzard.
What do they find here
that is alive, that counts
for sustenance?

Later they rise,
each bird an exclamation,
until the whole flock
moves as one unruly urge
towards heaven, ragged
and raucous as need always is.
The field's no emptier now
than before, but feels
the stillness in every clod,
the loss in every furrow.

Lee Robinson

November on the Ranch

Gritty blizzard rolls
      tumbleweeds . . . cattle shudder
        one pale rose shatters

Roberta Pipes Bowman

Windmill Song

Get up, wind!
Spin my wheel
of galvanized steel
looming
over cedar and oak.
Turn my shaft,
my gears. Plunge
my rods down
until the leathers cup
my joints and swell
and suck
the gyppy water up
a hundred up
two hundred feet
from vulgar limestone,
shale, marl.

Pull, would you, wind!
Through the buried pipe
and out the stem
this hard water surges
in the burning afternoon,
mingling in a concrete reservoir
with old rain and new,
gravity
feeding it
to trough my thirsty goats.

Or lay low, wind!
I don't care!
Just rock these blades a little.
I'll sing a slow,
bitching song
for feral hogs
lapping up the stars.

Robert A. Ayres

Feast of the Seven Sorrows

In the spectacle of heat near Corpus Christi,
where the cotton withers into bloom,
flashing its dry white fists, we curtain off
our southern bedrooms from the broad day
as if in illness or foreclosure.

Too hot to touch or bicker, we roll away
from one another and will not sleep.
Everything collapses like bad rage
or abandoned cars, and grief is what it is.
It clarifies on our tongues like salt.

Soon waiting becomes a religion of sorts,
and I look to the Feast of the Seven Sorrows
as a kind of union, summer to winter.
When the rain comes, we take it for a fire,
a blaze of needles over the wet street.

It trickles down the throats of gutters,
along the walls of rooms we wake to, hushed,
congealing into our flesh like snails.
They too go out to meet it, fire to fire,
trailing their bright secretions.

They climb our windows, their heads weaving
like blind musicians, and the world burns
down to its blue glass. We rise to it,
the way a wound rises into pain and higher
into talk and the memory of pain,

the way water rises in our gardens and tongues,
how we eye the steamed breasts of birds.
We open them with knives and blessings rising
to occasions. We pity them, the bodiless
wings. We take them to our lips and moan.

                              Bruce Bond

Rain on the Plains

Rain brings the smell of spilled honey. Here
place is elemental: wind, sun, dirt,
rain. The mountains, now veiled in shadow, fill
with memories. Thunder takes voice
like the passing of a train. Our words
are blown back into their cave. Each day we watch
new age spots rise—chips of a skeleton
we will never see.

Here air changes the color of things. The plains
roll out smooth as gingerbread: reddish
with too much spice. Lightning lights
the desert and ancestors murmur
as they walk through the pass to the north
the pure murmur of life.

Everything fills with light. Aren't we like that: flash,
and then, gone? We illuminate our landscape
where our cells say, "Yes. Here. Yes."

Solana DeLámant

Music Box

Christmas morning I get up at five a.m. to drive
to San Antonio. I'm a nurse; my children are far away.
I'm working so others can be with their families.

I leave town on damp, shadowy streets
Dickens might have written into *A Christmas Carol.*
Inspiration crunches under my tires. Festive is a sleepy word.

Adoramus Te, Christe hums from the radio,
turns my car into a Hill Country music box. Alone
in the dark, I feel potential dawn licking me awake.

166

In windows, decorated trees invite light. Behind them
the sleepless unwrap good-byes in bright packages
tied tight with ribbons of knotted years.

I am the only celebrant of the present. Cellos sing me
down the road. Sopranos and guitars voice my prayers:
may deer stay nested beneath mesquite. May coyotes

and armadillos seek food only on their side of the road.
What did Mary know about clouds of sound rising up and up?
She knew her response to God's riff, His call for a reprise.

She knew the world could heal when every creature sings.
Over the hill, a bright star approaches at eighty miles an hour.
Did wise men see a similar blurred vision of light in the sky?

My hands grip the wheel. The truck and I approach, pass.
All-out brights. The Voice of the Hill Country drives me
toward morning. My racing heart meets God in a grace note.

Lianne Elizabeth Mercer

Winter Sunlight

for Elwood and JoAnn Meischen

Life begins at any age, the surprise
of it sudden as a blue norther sweeping
the landscape clean, nothing between here
and the North Pole but a single strand of barbed
wire: a sky so clear with sunlight we forget the gray
that hunkers down, that will not give us room to breathe,
the hush at bedtime heavy as the grave that takes
from us love's healing breath, leaves us alone
to count the days we cannot fill with light
until love comes again and
touches us with warmth.

David Meischen

Charmed by Hurricanes

Tired of everything known,
charmed by the word *hurricane*,
Emily decides to try one,
ties herself to a sturdy tree.

Her Botticelli-faced neighbor,
rolling a baby on her hip
like a pearl on half-shell, begs:
*Evacuate with us. You sweet,
demented Northerner.*
Oblivious to words, Emily
watches the woman's eyebrows,
pencil-drawn and false as today's
postcard-blue, planetarium-calm sky.

In the Gulf, angry hula hoops spin,
twirling an ocean around a hurricane's eye.
Soon she'll see what others tell. How pine
trees snap to arrows and sea rain drives
through wood. How wind masticates leaves
to pulp, molds sculptures of miscellaneous things.

Emily loves a storm, pursues personal
definitions. Wants them clear as the day
lightning flashed in her kitchen, turned
her hand numb as the lemon she peeled.
She wonders how it will feel, pressed
into a tree trunk, covered in God's green
tobacco, thrown by His mud-pie hand.

Carolyn A. Dahl

Winter in the Panhandle

Remember the cold time. October surprised,
glazed the hay with ice. November posted
freeze warnings, later nailed us with sleet.

The barn steamed with cow's breath
and reeked of dung. Pumps heaved ice
before gales from the Rockies sent

cattle searching for shelter. Kerosene torched
kindling in the wood stove. Don't forget January
sent blizzards, muffled our world in snow, held

us captive without power. After the snow ceased
we scraped the stock pond and skated. At sunrise
the rooster raised a ruckus from the top of the barn.

Watchman of our days, oldest of the flock,
the old bird knew we had to be at the north gate
when the yellow school bus chugged up the hill.

ELIZABETH S. BRATTEN

WHERE THE FIELDS LIE SERE AND FURROWED (GHAZAL FOR A JANUARY AFTERNOON)

after Patrick Kavanagh

Within winter light, a grayness grows
To draw us down, to call us back.

Your hands, turning the farther landscape.
Your voice, the chill upon distance.

I lost my way this morning—the snow
settled. I thought I'd know the road.

Give me absolutes now: crows that pass
overhead in autumn . . . . They fill

the brittled trees. Motion. Water. Slow
islands. Grief, be a falling leaf.

STEVE WILSON

169

Cedar Fever

The effects: twelve sneezes over coffee
Trash cans stuffed
With sodden Kleenex, wads of tears
Hot streams
Trickling down the cheeks
Itching in the throat
That speaking doesn't scratch.

The cause: green flames
Shooting up brown hillsides
In the worst of January
Spiked emeralds erupting
From the miles
And miles
Of winter.

Smoldering by farm-to-market roads
They jump blacktops everywhere
A blaze
That speaks a hundred pungent tongues
And climbs
Into gray skies
To heat the coldest afternoon.

Carol Coffee Reposa

High Noon and Texas Beckons

New England 2005

I collect the rocks from
beneath the snow. Their refusal
to freeze intrigues

and encourages me. Blue,
I question this northern sky—
breath coiled and scattered

by the lips of a god I've never known.
Frigid beads, in every brutal form,
slam my face and children.

This black noon, I remember
the fervor of the dripping sun:
childhood in bare feet,

watermelon on ice, tomatoes
off the vine; peach jelly melted
and swallowed by the thirsty white cotton

of my grandmother's apron; the rousing
scent of brushfire in the barren roast
of my kind of season.

I carry her dry earth in my mouth.

LAURIE A. GUERRERO

ONE IN EVERY YEAR

Now August is her summer self again
in high-heeled shoes, her dress a blistering red.
She breathes her torch and steals to center stage;
her presence we endure but never trust
because for nature she must play her role.
With flair upon the altar of our fields,
once more she seals the fate of thirsting crops,
ignoring pleas, returning them to dust
from which they came. We watch as sun descends,
another day survived. Soon evening wind
reminds us all that fall will meet our needs.
We're older now, aware of August's game.
At season's end, with style she'll thumb her nose
in waves of heat then hitch a ride outbound.

NAOMI STROUD SIMMONS

Seasons in the Doorways

In the doorways the scene is changing. Piece by piece,
pumpkins and scarecrows fade away into pine wreaths
and poinsettias. The year rolls out to its end,
on strings of lights and candles.

It is a season of bees. One stings my hand,
displacing my theory that nature knows I love it
and accepts my terms of peace. It will send
bees and winter when it will.

In this place of doorways, bit by bit,
we let go of what we thought we understood,
and open as wide as we can hope.

Margie McCreless Roe

Live Oak

Mexican fires grit the sky.
Sun flashes off Zippos
swinging on chains. This is not
the beautiful season.

The honey of yucca blooms
ended months ago:
the bluebonnet interstates
recede, a burnt mosaic.

The dark-leafed local scrub
is called "live" oak
because no one else's trees
could live here.

The Guadalupe is greener
than the grass, blurry
with fat water moccasins.
August rots everything.

Envelopes stick to themselves
like foreigners
who don't speak the language.
Coffee pours like molasses.

This is the time of lightning.
Only rattlesnakes hunt
in this heat, sucking water
from the bones of mice.

RACHEL BARENBLAT

BRADFORD PEARS IN SPRING

Blossoms thick as wool
hide delicate buds

from the icy teeth
of spring wind,

trumpet the birth
of a new season,

not with glorious shouts
but in whispers

of white against
the blue enamel

of skies laced
with sun-worn clouds,

tattered reminders
of winter's bluster

at the inevitable pace
of revival.

DR. CHARLES A. STONE

On Reading *The Shipping News* in Houston in August

My Yankee uncles called it *Hooston* after a Boston street.
Those days you had to say the state
along with the city's name or risk blank looks.
We came from Ohio, innocent, transferred—
no mention of the tropics, that hardship pay
was what the British Consul got in this barely
heard-of place, as if it were Calcutta.
Marooned in an upstairs apartment
with an old metal fan and no car
I thought I would dissolve like the witch in *The Wizard of Oz*.

Forty-seven summers here still haven't
thinned my blood. I shudder from the heat.
But now I'm dreaming of Newfoundland—
endless miles of untouched snow,
frozen, soundless streets, blue winds,
and crags of silver ice, the deepest cold—
yearning for that other kind of heat,
a slow fire, some English tea,
a pot of thick soup waiting on the stove.

CATHY STERN

385 North

The monthly pilgrimage to Lubbock, Texas
waltzed onto box twelve of the
September slot. Dusk was the target
but dinner, other errands, procrastination
overshot the mark into a
thick still darkness on 385 North.
Distance and music waxed,
constant companions.
Stars wrapped around themselves
in a sullen night sky; the absence of

street lights exaggerated a halo of brilliance.
Over my steering-wheel, the moon
rode on my hood. I drove unappreciative
of its offerings.

The calendar that dictated my journey
remains hesitant to pronounce season changes.
Yet grass along the route has already
retired for the summer, cotton fields recede
and a single tree, absent of autumn's colors,
stands wrestling with summer.
Its proud green leaves will soon inherit shades
of orange and brown, and the genes of balding
will dominate, and
when winter waltzes onto one of the boxes,
like me, that tree will stand alone, bare,
naked beneath a rich night sky.

LORETTA DIANE WALKER

His Grownup Lullaby

The sound he loved, our grandpa said,
Was rain on a tin roof overhead.
He used to wait some warm spring night
To hear the drops come soft and light.
He relished, too, a lightning flash
With rain that roared, crash after crash,
But winter-warm and snug inside
When stormy rains lashed far and wide,
He lay and smiled and heard their proof
Of music on his old tin roof.
The rolling drums' deep steady din,
The wind's cello against the tin,
The night's own turbulence on high
That made his grownup lullaby.

VIOLETTE NEWTON

First Cold Snap at the Ranch

Summer weekends I drag the garden hose downhill
through poison oak, yucca, an occasional slithering snake
to overflow murky water in the concrete tanks.

With the first cold snap, slimy green moss
retreats to the water's edge, then disappears.
Wasps, skater bugs, saffron butterflies,
pollywogs vanish into frigid air.
Dirt and muck settle firmly on the bottom
and what remains above shines clear
as a pane of polished glass.

I lift a floating twig, a single copper leaf
hear a cricket like a tiny bell ring out
from live oaks at the field's edge
and wonder at the ease with which
a gray, furrowed sky, a wind that shrieks
can clear the wretched mess life makes of things.

Patricia Spears Bigelow

It Rains When It Rains and Rains

It rains and rains
When it rains in South Texas
And it rains. Or it
Doesn't at all. Any

Questions? Not in the cobwebs,
Not in the scattered dust
Pocked on umbrellas dug out
And leaking over drenched heads.

No questions among the insects
Washed down the ditches
Settled as dry land.
No, when it rains, it rains

And rains in South Texas,
And there's no doubt about drenching,
And there's no doubt we ignored
The shingles too long as it rains

And the rain doesn't stop in South Texas
Because after thinking, cogitating,
Clogging so long, it feels, it feels,
Yes, so good to rain and rain.

DAVID BREEDEN

Reunion

The trees told her. One year after Hurricane Rita, few stood. Not erect but bent back like bows. Arrows for limbs. Others were decapitated, two branches pointing outward like black arms on a clock making the trees even in wind, silent. An old pine stripped of the color green except for a few veins of Asian jasmine daring to creep up its trunk. Bamboo that once served as a lush green fence line, stood plucked, like a family of toothpicks at angles evoking alarm. Still in shock from the storm.

When she entered the house, she immediately felt enveloped. It was as if the house knew that she was coming, had been waiting for her return. She stood wrapped in a wetness not from weather. It dripped down the walls as if the house was still weeping from their sudden departure long ago. An entire family, dismembered from its place, in some ways as violently as Hurricane Rita had uprooted the trees.

She walked from window to window opening grateful draperies. Some seemed to sigh in relief, others resisting whispered to her, "Please, try again, pull gently." Every room she entered with reverence, gently running her fingers along the walls like they were sunburned skin. "The house wants breath," she thought, "it needs to breathe." She wanted to carefully crack it open like an egg, spread the wall-paper out smooth and study it like a map, tracing the veins of a life that once lived there. Still did.

KATIE OXFORD

Blue Norther

Halfway from Abilene to Lubbock,
And halfway through November,
We steered right on a red map-squiggle—
A road replaced by faster asphalt lined with faster food—
A long gray snake of a road, lying like a shed skin
In dun grass bent and crippled by raw winds.
We drove, saluted by peeling billboards for motels long abandoned,
By ragged fence posts marking the miles, and rusted wire,
But no other cars, no cattle even,
As if the dishrag sky sifting down to the yellow grass,
As if the desolation was ours alone.
Riding fence line in my thoughts, cheek against the chill car window,
I saw it before the radio snapped and growled a weather warning:
Arctic front, a real blue norther.

It was not sudden. It did not come down like a curtain.
It was simply there, as if it had always been our destination:
A wall of blue—yes, blue—a monument, an arctic wing
Sweeping the horizon from our road,
A strange, thick-shadowed blue:
Deep water, full of unnamed things,
The color of cold.

Like divers jumping in, I think we took a breath
Before we drove into it, into the blue,
Disappearing under the hem of winter's veil,
Heading north, to find its teeth.

Karen Cecile Moon

Galveston Waits

I know the history here, how pressures can
send the sea to claim its right of land.
I don't understand how a low wall
can alter weather's wrath.

Gulls fly unconcerned; other birds nestle
among wildflowers that bloom on grassy dunes
whose roots hold on to what they can.
Out at the end of narrow asphalt lifelines

tall hotels challenge the southern seas.
Houses stand on legs like herons at rest.
But herons and gulls can fly away;
these square tethered bodies stare out to sea—

odd birds of wood and glass
whose legs are pile-driven deep in the ground,
huddled together as if numbers assure safety.

MARGARET ELLIS HILL

May

It hasn't in years but if spring
lasts even a month this time
it will happen in May when winecups bloom,
when purple thistles rise
near the tiny vervain,

when at this place where three winds meet
Indian blanket and Mexican hat
sway beneath overcast skies
with sawtooth daisies and buttercups,
brown-eyed Susans and dock.

If spring lasts even a month
it will happen in May when winds
become breezes, if it happens at all,
it will happen in May when the world
flares open its petals,

its wild little mouths loud with hymns.

JAMES HOGGARD

The 'Fraidy Hole

The root cellar was dark and damp,
a place to hide when skies convulsed
and thunder rumbled in the roiling clouds.
        It was our dirt floor sanctuary,
where cobwebs hung from ceiling boards
and hairy spiders spun nightmares in our heads.
We called it the 'fraidy hole.

Living in Tornado Alley, land of Texas twisters,
we learned to watch the weather,
listen to the levels of alert with growing fear.
Tornado watch.
        Tornado warning.
                Tornado down.

Mother opened all the windows
so the house would not explode.
My job was to grab the flashlight
and rush my little brother to the basement.
        We sat curled against the wall,
                terrified and waiting for the worst.
Father brought the battery-powered radio
and we listened to its raspy warnings.

Our house was never touched by a tornado,
but every time the warning came we named
the last one in the the 'fraidy hole the bravest.
I never received that honor.

CLAIRE OTTENSTEIN-ROSS

October Song

After a summer that nearly
burned us to ash, a cool wind
blew in and then three days of
steady rain. The skeletal rose

bushes drank heavily and deep,
uncurled withering roots and
put out an October burst of
bloom. The basil too rebounded
and the air spiced with smells.
There was a happiness of bees.
Monarchs passed through, off
to Mexico without bag or visa.
Last night, it all exploded.
Rose petals, red ones and pink,
carpet the ground as though a
secret wedding happened in
the dark. Three small mockingbird
feathers are pinned under the
barrage of acorns that pelt anyone
walking under the oak.
I'm office bound and restless.
I want to be somewhere
tossed, exploding,
losing feathers
in a flurry of breath
and song and heat.

BEVERLY VOSS

CONTENTMENT

A norther has roared down from Amarillo
turning the sky gray.
On the lake, anhingas scatter in the gale,
long necks straining in frantic flight.
A pot of chili is simmering,
filling the kitchen with onion and cumin.
I ladle it up and call you to the table,
grateful for this moment of grace.
Others may crave a loaf of bread and jug of wine.
All I want on this cold winter day
is you, a box of crackers and a bowl of Texas Red.

SHELLIE LYON

Late Winter in San Antonio

All kinds of darkness weigh me down.
Gray flannel sky swaddles the sun
and I sit fixed like furniture
in my dim house where corners sigh
and shift in shadows.

But some blind force draws me out
into air thick as bolts of tulle
that shrink my view of a backyard
sodden with rotten progeny
of summer's blossoms.
Things as they'll be at the end:
stumps, mud, shreds—
oozing excuses for life—
too much water, too little light.

Then, to my left, almost unseen,
the south wall's offering,
an orange rose glowing
on spotted stems
among tattered leaves.

Marian Aitches

El Paso

The sun spilled
relentless.
Thin white blood
soaking everything
day and half the night.

Hard blue days
so bright
the mountain
bronzed.

One year
they planted poppies
via a soaring
yellow crop duster
that dropped clouds
of dark seeds
over the mountain.
We hoped for flowering
slopes in the spring.

No rain.
No flowers.

Just one damn beautiful day
after another.

Doris Duncan

Middle of Summer

Two boys in the garden, playing

Follow the Leader a few rows back—
they laughed, tumbled through lantana,
leapfrogged from bed to bed. Churning up

dirt I'd smoothed under my trowel,
their hands rooted into the loam
for worms, fat white grubs, beetles.

Breathless with energy, joyous, faces full
to the warmth, they drew down sun,
these boys, as they set out for home single-file,

felling larkspur, roses, zinnias on their way.

Steve Wilson

In South Texas

Snow sheathes Spanish daggers
       splits blue piñatas
       covers ripened oranges
       spreads over bare fields
       It reflects in street lamps
       decorates strings of red lights
       fashions white fans from palm leaves
       and keeps excited children up all night
Snow falls on Christmas Eve
       for the first time in a hundred years

Lynn Edge

Influenza

I have lain on this couch
for two weeks now,
staring out
at the bleak landscape
of this Texas winter.

A tree in my yard
has lost all but three
of its yellowed leaves.
I have watched as gusts of wind came
and claimed them.

Staccato branches
pierce the sky,
with its endless movie
of transforming cloud shapes—
now gray, now white, now peach.

Birds, in small flocks,
fly past my window.
An occasional car creeps by
on the open road.

I see the twisted trunks of trees
embrace the silence,
and witness the dying light of day
drag its golden cloak over
my neighbor's wall.

SALLY ALTER

ICE STORM

One autumn after days of rain, a norther blew in just past dawn
as if two pewter palms had clamped down on our patch of earth
stoppering wind, rain and light. Our sopping world plunged into chill
and froze entire: each branch and twig, each strand of grass
The clumps of clods beside our road, the arc of wires strung pole to pole
Every thing beneath that sky shimmered with a gloss of ice

We walked out into nearby woods of papershell and blackjack trees
Each step crunched underneath our feet like walking over broken bulbs
The clank of frosted tubes threw tinkling notes into the gaps
between each tree, and when we brushed against a branch, some sleeves
would slip onto the ground in piles like beakers thrown away
I heard no birds and wondered where they hid today. I was afraid
if I looked too close at upper limbs, perhaps I'd see
their rigid bodies clustered like a gelid fruit with open eyes

I was too young to have a guess that this might be the only time
I'd ever see this kind of freeze, given where I map my years
My coat was corduroy, unlined, and I had not brought gloves or hat
My breath blew out in cheerful clouds, and I cannot recall a thing
we said to one another. We did not touch, we had not yet begun
to touch. You stopped once and I came back to see what might
have drawn your gaze. You turned to face me and I had the thought
that maybe we would kiss. But I was young in that way, too
So I turned and went on in the woods

MAGGIE JOCHILD

Spring Returns to an Ever-Urbanizing Texas

In town the redbuds blaze in the yards
like Persian fireworks. The oak trees,
having dropped the year's last load of leaves,
are hung with fuzzy pollen at the green end
of chartreuse. Whether or not we had winter
we have spring.

Out here the freeway cuts range land
no good for much but grazing, though sometimes
there's a little oil. The groves of trash trees,
let run to hold the gumbo till developers
say it's time, swarm with a haze of gold
just beyond budding—so sweet you forget
the brutalities of heat to come
and smile.

The lights at the end of the ramp
are wound with sack cloth.
Men in jeans and rubber boots
scrape a curve of puddled earth
to widen the interchange.

Sun lavishes itself on new grass,
Crayola green, green as lime Life Savers.

In the lot at Baybrook Mall
somebody's chance-nudged car alarm
chirps like a bird.

John Gorman

Weekend Forecast

One day we will dine slowly and well,
just the two of us, talking about books,
remembering paintings from the afternoon

at the museum, remarking in passing
about what one of the children might have said
if he had walked one of the corridors with us
and had not caused a commotion and left us
embarrassed, apologetic, defeated.
We will share a little Pinot Noir,
but not so much I grow tiresome and dark.
There will be a hotel, not some traveler's lodge,
with a large room—TV hidden behind
latched oak doors—a deep tub and wide, firm bed,
big windows, undraped, far above neon
and noise, where I will unrobe you for angels
to see. So please forgive me this year
if committees, contracts, sleet, and chicken pox
have made me a man who mumbles distant
promises about a quiet late lunch,
a slow drive beside the river back home,
azaleas pink and tangled upon the rise.

Lyman Grant

The Ghost of Autumn Past

While
surrounded by bricks and concrete at a bus stop
downtown, and
enduring the labor pangs of the city's first
truly genuine
cold front,
you realize that your heart is buried
beneath a pine-tree-colored hill that
once grew your Big Daddy's watermelons,
and it
knows
that it's way too soon to kill hogs,
but we will still need a fire tonight.

Lynn Lewis

Texas Roots

Life here must be more creative;
it has much to overcome:
floods, droughts, hail,
the probing finger of the tornado.

But in the end
floods sweep clean,
droughts toughen the earth, and
hail thins the weak from the hardy.

The tornado is but a scouring
wind chasing a vacuum
across the plains;
there is no anger in it.

This morning, under the first blush
of a purple dawn, a grackle
perched on the crosspiece of my grille
to pluck butterflies, still warm,
from the hot mouth of my radiator.

And in the stillness of virgin daylight,
the sinuous roots of this land
rose entwining from the ground,
to plunge with a sigh into my heart.

                              John Brooks

Eighteen Days on the Ground

Can it be more than twenty years and still they speak
of snow that stayed so long upon the ground?
Eighteen days, they say, as if it just occurred.
Any snow at all is rare in northeast Texas.
When it comes, it comes and goes so quickly
that it seems a dream. But not that year, in 1983.
It came and stayed, and froze into a dirty ice

that gripped imagination in a vise from which
they could not free themselves. Only tongues
thawed and said over and over how long
it stayed. Folks tottered on the frozen ground
as they walked around discussing snow
with neighbors just as shocked as they.
My parents had a picture window six feet wide
through which they stared for eighteen days
as if they watched a marathon of old sitcoms.
I suppose it was the wonder of it all, one-time
phenomenon, that made this story last. I smile
at what I tell, and that I tell it once again.

LINDA BANKS

DROUGHT

Another rainless cold front,
winds coming all the way from Canada
just to tease and suck what
little moisture may be in the grass.

Sparks from trains start fires,
whipped to a frenzy by cold, dry gusts.
The world is an orgy of fire, bands
of flaming grass north and south and west.

Tonight the news is full of burning
barns and trailer parks, tearful housewives
showing off ruined photographs,
a family picking through the rubble of a home.

Out beyond the edge of town, harbingers
that worse is yet to come: cracked, parched soil,
stock ponds shrinking to a muddy core,
signs at churches telling us to pray for rain
under sere skies of relentless blue.

RALPH HAUSSER

The Pecan Trees

The last leaves have given up,
limbs laid bare as driftwood,
the gray of winter creeks.

The yard is littered with small branches,
broken fingers, crooked, cracked.
I never see them fall—never!—

but there they are, strewn
across the ashen grass,
the debris of abandoned resolutions.

Bent low to the earth,
I gather and clear them—
leaves, twigs, all the dead things

that have collected around me—
testaments to December's end,
the prayers of another year.

Scott Wiggerman

Storm Warning

. . . sustained winds near one hundred ten . . .
En masse, we boarded up windows, cleared
grocery shelves of bottled water, batteries,
calmed the children,

. . . heavy flooding expected . . .
recalled television scenes of people cramming
into shelters, eating Red Cross dinners,
sleeping on cement floors, returning to splintered
homes and waterlogged possessions,

. . . moving rapidly toward the Texas coastline . . .
scanned the growing gray above us, gathered
most beloved belongings, joined
bumper-to-bumper traffic fleeing northward;

. . . estimated time of arrival: early evening . . .
then, in unison, we shuddered—the somber
sounding newscaster unaware the storm
had already made landfall in our hearts.

Lounell Whitaker

Turning of the Blackgum

Over sun-wallowed pavement
and along a verge of forest
where the Big Lake
riffles its prowess
and frets like a summer's child,
the blackgum tree
holds autumn at bay
with taut arms,
and blood drips
from its fingertips.

A leaf falls, and somewhere
wild poppies bloom again
on scarred hills
and along barbed banks
and on white-crossed meadows
of familiar names.

I shudder
at the transparency
of a red leaf, falling.

Evelyn Corry Appelbee

Fall Foliage

for Ruby Jo

In October, Hill Country
leaves startle the senses
with color—amber, salmon,

rose to red and downright yellow.
Trees quilt the mountains
and crayola the roadsides.

You would breathe the air,
crisp as a new deck of cards,
pull out your calendar, ask,

"When can we play, huh?"
Remember, we played
bridge in Galveston, admired

the lights next door, the way
they hovered above the water,
not your gaudy red, green

and blue ones, but soft, somehow
European in feeling, golds, mauves
and an occasional red. Made

us think of villas and dukes
and exotic evenings. Ruby,
Ruby Jo, where will we get

a fourth for odd jokes, for
bidding fights, someone who
understands the clarity of color?

U. T. Abercrombie

Weather: The First Year

*for my mother, Jewel Bruner, who moved to the
top of Mt. Barry Scobee, outside Ft. Davis, in 1980*

In bitter storm the rock-sized hail
attacked the new roof, dented the truck,
battered the poor-will protecting her young
to a rubble of feathers.
As soon as the skin of the house was air-tight
a blizzard descended, severed electricity's
lifeline climbing through silence.

She camped out indoors, her comfort
the fresh-papered walls, still-breathing plants,
some tropicals in greenhouse glass.
But they blackened, froze.
People below said, "Unusual. That early
we never have snow." She had chosen
a world of exceptions.

On the day of the big blow, wind on the mountain
topped its highest recorded speed. (God knows
how fast it had blown in the eons
before humans poked instruments toward stars,
when agave arrived, or the mountains lifted.)
Wind bowed the glass door; she leaned against it,
furious that nature would crack her new work.

Arms braced, one woman eye to eye
with the wind, she won.
It was part luck, part spirit, and ignorance
of what she was up against.
In the raptured stillness after, she found a table,
thick pine it took two strong men to budge,
tossed to another part of the slope.

Del Marie Rogers

Tell-tale

Winter reveals
Hawks perched, preening, pausing
Between pitch and plunge,
Disclosing the other life of birds,
The kernel of nest and nurture,
Shell and quill.

In splintered candor
Betraying summer's seclusions
Winter tattles that flight
Is rooted on a hard hill.

Mike Carter

Two Hours in Fall

It is fall and we are laughing
laughing ourselves into leaves
falling into ourselves over the floor
something about the word flinging
flinging our words out to the world like blown leaves
flinging something our mothers would never allow
but it is fall so we are flinging ourselves
off walls   over waterfalls   into the sea
and when we begin
to settle down
a Cooper's hawk flies in
between the jabber of mockingbirds
flings itself on the fence not two feet
from the window and we thrill in the fall
at this blessing—
become quiet and cool in hawk's presence
not on edge at all
flung out—

Perie Longo

194

Norther

That winter
the boys' jeans
froze on the clothesline.

The norther blew in so hard, so fast,
Momma yanked them off the line,
but couldn't get 'em dry.

The boys laughingly
wore the wet denim
into the orchard to prune
and brush creosote on the
limbs they'd amputated earlier.

Home for dinner at noon,
they wiggled out of the wet britches.
Sat at the table in their underdrawers,
joking about who had the best legs.
Feasted on thick slices of ham, black-eyed peas,
hot biscuits and red-eye gravy,
Aunt Litie's preserves.

The jeans dried before the fireplace
as they dozed, dreaming of warmth.

Hot peach cobbler was ready
to devour before they returned
to the orchard in warm jeans
and bellies full of summer.

Robin Cate

Contributor Notes & Index

V. T. Abercrombie has published in *Home Planet News, Roanoke Review, White Rock Review, Slant, Madison Review, Pudding, Rockhurst Review, Pleiades, Borderlands, Illya's Honey, Visions International, Main Street Rag*, and several anthologies, including *The Weight of Addition*. Her book, *Luminist*, is forthcoming from Black Buzzard Press. (106, 134, 192)

Kaye Voigt Abikhaled was editor and publisher from 1999 to 2004 of *A Galaxy of Verse*, a biannual poetry journal. She was the local Chair for Poetry in Schools for five years and State Chair from 2002 to 2003. Her published poetry books include *Club des Poètes, Lyrics of Lebanon*, and *Childhood in the Third Reich: World War II and Its Aftermath*, of which she also authored a bilingual edition in German with the same title. (68, 93)

Carolyn Adams' art and poetry have been published in *HazMat Review, The Alembic, Mad Hatters Review, Mannequin Envy, The Weight of Addition*, and *Foliate Oak*, among others. She is the author of the chapbook *Beautiful Strangers* (Lily Press, 2006) and of the art web chapbook *What Do You See?*, published by Right Hand Pointing and available for free download. (130)

Marian Aitches is a professor in the History Department at the University of Texas in San Antonio, where she specializes in American Indian history. She is working on a memoir/history of Victoria Courts, the San Antonio public housing projects where she grew up. (182)

Deb Akers was born in Louisiana, raised in Texas and has lived in Austin since the early 70's. Her work has been published in a variety of media, most recently in *farfelu magazine*. A long-time volunteer and board member for the Austin International Poetry Festival, she served as the 2008 AIPF chairman and edits its yearly youth poetry anthology, *Diverse Youth*. She presently serves as the board chair for *Borderlands: Texas Poetry Review*. (53)

Sally Alter is past editor of *Illuminations*, Schreiner University's international e-journal. Her poetry has been published in *The Muse* and *The Kerrville Daily Times*, as well as Houston and Austin poetry anthologies. She is a member of the Kerrville Writers Association and The Kerrville Novel Writers Association. Born in England, she now lives in Texas where she is currently working on a poetry manuscript and a contemporary suspense novel. (57, 184)

Evelyn Corry Appelbee is a native Texan and author of *Let Rocks Their Silence Break*, winner of the eighth annual Nortex Press Book Award,

sponsored by the Poetry Society of Texas. Living on thirty acres in the beautiful Piney Woods of East Texas, she is the author of seven books of prose and poetry and recipient of the Hilton Ross Greer Outstanding Service Award. In 2007, she was nominated for Poet Laureate of Texas. (191)

Robert A. Ayres has contributed poems to the anthologies *Is This Forever, or What?, Four Way Reader #2, Urban Nature*, and *Outsiders*, as well as literary journals and magazines. He received his MFA from the Warren Wilson Program for Writers. A native of San Antonio, he lives in Austin, where he is actively involved in efforts to promote land stewardship and conservation. (164)

Valerie Martin Bailey has earned the San Antonio Poets Association's title of poet laureate seven times and has earned their Poetic Excellence Award five times. She has been SAPA's publication chair and editor of *Inkwell Echoes* for 24 years. A member of the National Federation of State Poetry Societies, Bailey serves as editor of its national anthology, *The Encore*. She has published two books of poetry, *A Gathering of Roses* and *Spinning Straw into Gold*. (126)

Rebecca Balcárcel holds an MFA from Bennington College and teaches creative writing at Tarrant County College in Hurst, Texas. Daughter of an Anglo mother and a Guatemalan father, she explores her bicultural upbringing in her work. Rebecca's adventures include mothering three boys, skydiving, and seeing the Sistine Chapel in 2008. (84)

Linda Banks was born in Red River County, Texas, and lived there until she married and moved to the Dallas area over forty years ago. She loves to travel and gather inspiration for exotic poems with a homegrown flavor, reflected in her love of gardening. She is a Life Member of the Poetry Society of Texas, where she has made many life-long friends and received inspiration and guidance for her own writing. (100, 108, 188)

Rachel Barenblat is a student in the ALEPH rabbinic program and author of three poetry chapbooks—most recently *chaplainbook*, a collection of hospital chaplaincy poems from Laupe House Press. She holds an MFA from Bennington and is associate editor at *Zeek*, a Jewish journal of thought and culture. In 2008, Velveteen Rabbi, her blog about Judaism and poetry, was named one of the top 25 blogs in the world by *Time*. (172)

Adam Berlin is the author of the novels *Belmondo Style* (St. Martin's Press, 2004), which won The Publishing Triangle's 2005 Ferro-Grumley Award for best novel, and *Headlock* (Algonquin Books, 2000). His stories and poetry have appeared in numerous journals. He is an Assistant Professor of English at John Jay College of Criminal Justice in New York City and co-editor of *J Journal: New Writing on Justice*. (138)

Diane Gonzales Bertrand is Writer-in-Residence at St. Mary's University in San Antonio. Her poetry has been published in a variety of Texas journals and newspapers. Her award-winning books for children and teens include *Trino's Choice, The Ruiz Street Kids, The Empanadas That Abuela Made,* and *We are Cousins/Somos Primos.* (8)

Patricia Spears Bigelow has had poetry in various anthologies, including *Is This Forever, or What?* and *Bless the Beasts.* Her collection *Midnight Housekeeping* (Riverlily Press) was published in 2003. (120, 176)

Alan Birkelbach's work has appeared in journals such as *Borderlands* and *Concho River Review.* He has four collections of poetry: *Bone Song, Weighed in the Balances, No Boundaries,* and *Alan Birkelbach: New and Selected Works.* In 2005 the Texas Legislature chose Birkelbach as the Texas State Poet Laureate. (31, 75)

Suzanne Blair, of Batesville, Arkansas, is an essayist and poet with work published in both the United States and England. She is also a freelance reviewer and member of the National Book Critics Circle. (46)

Joe Blanda, originally from Orange, Texas, is a singer-songwriter, poet, and technical editor. Technical editing pays the mortgage; music and poetry pay the bills that pile up in his psyche. His CDs of original songs include *The Moon in the Man* and *Acoustic Muse.* (50)

Toby Leah Bochan received her MFA from the Michener Center for Writers at the University of Texas in Austin. She is the author of *The Badass Girls' Guide to Poker* and currently runs the poker site for About.com. She lives in New York with her husband, Matt. (82)

Bruce Bond's most recent collections of poetry include *Blind Rain* (LSU, 2008), *Cinder* (Etruscan Press, 2003), and *The Throats of Narcissus* (University of Arkansas, 2001). His poetry has appeared in *Best American Poetry, The Yale Review, The Georgia Review, Raritan, Poetry,* and other journals. He is a Regents Professor of English at the University of North Texas and Poetry Editor for *American Literary Review.* (165)

Lana Book lives at the Hill Country Sculpture and Meditation Garden in the Texas Hill Country near Kerrville. She writes about common situations and emotions, often with a twist that surprises the reader. Writing doesn't always come easy for her, perhaps because she writes about things that matter to her, which can sometimes be difficult. She wants to leave something behind that says, "That was who she was." (12)

Ann Reisfeld Boutté is an award-winning writer of poems, essays, and feature stories. She has an MA in Journalism from American University and has been feature writer for both a daily newspaper and a national news service. She was a Juried Poet in the Houston Poetry Fest in 2001 and 2005. (22, 42, 86)

Roberta Pipes Bowman is the author of eight books of poetry, one of which won the Lucidity Chapbook Award. Twice nominated for Poet Laureate of Texas and once for a Pushcart Prize, Bowman has won several poetry awards. She has had short stories in *Suddenly* and poems in *descant* and *Aries.* Her book, *From Flour Sacks to Satin,* the story of a blind sharecropper's daughter during the twenties and thirties, was published in March 2008. (163)

Mary Ellen Branan, PhD, took up studying poetry at middle age at the University of Houston's Creative Writing Program. She now lives in Bastrop, hoping to win big publications and contests. (156)

Martha Everhart Braniff's *Songs from the Bone Closet* (Stone River Press) was a finalist for the 2004 Violet Crown Award for Literary Fiction and Poetry, and *Step over Rio* won the Writers' League of Texas' Mystery/Adventure Novel Award. She has been nominated for the Pushcart Prize for "Resurrection," a short story published in *Happy,* and an essay, "Voices Calling," published in *Raving Dove.* Her fiction, essays, and poetry have been widely published. (101, 140)

Elizabeth S. Bratten, a native of Georgia, is a charter member of The Friday Line, a Houston poetry workshop begun in the 1970's. (168)

David Breeden, aka Dr. Poetry, has an MFA from the Iowa Writers' Workshop and a PhD from the Center for Writers at the University of Southern Mississippi. He has published four novels and nine books of poetry and is a Unitarian Universalist minister. (176)

John Brooks is a retired IBM Project Manager and a former Marine with four grown children. He has been writing poetry most of his life, but seldom publishes. He prefers life through the eyes of a poet—a moth as an open book, daffodils as an inland sea, a cockroach as a loose skateboard skimming across the kitchen floor—and cannot imagine seeing the world any other way. He lives in Fort Worth, Texas, with his wife, Carol, and their Airedale, Maggie. (136, 188)

Andrea Hollander Budy's third full-length poetry collection is *Woman in the Painting* (Autumn House Press, 2006). Her honors include the Nicholas Roerich Poetry Prize, the D. H. Lawrence Fellowship, a Pushcart Prize, and two poetry fellowships from the National Endowment for the Arts. With poems in *Poetry, The Gettysburg Review, The Georgia Review, Shenandoah,* and *FIELD,* Budy has worked as Writer-in-Residence at Lyon College in Arkansas. (114)

Graham Burchell is the winner of the 2005 Chapter One Promotions Open Poetry Competition and the 2006 Hazel Street Productions Poetry Contest. He was nominated for a 2006 Pushcart Prize. His first two poetry collections came out in 2008—*Ladies of Divided Twins* (Erbacce Press) and *Vermeer's Corner* (Foothills Publishing). Currently living in his native England, he is the editor of the online poetry journal, *Words-Myth.* (87)

Robert Burlingame, an Emeritus Professor at the University of Texas, El Paso, has published four books/chapbooks, as well as poems in *Saturday Review, Texas Observer, Northwest Review, Pushcart Prize III, Bloomsbury Review, Southwest Review,* and others. He has appeared in over 35 regional, national, and international anthologies, including *Washing the Cow's Skull* and *The Weight of Addition.* He lives with his wife, Linda, on a ranch in the Guadalupe Mountains. (94)

Martha Kirby Capo won First Place in Poetry at the Houston Writers Conference 2000, was a featured reader at the Houston Poetry Fest 2001, and was named *Sol Magazine's* Poet Laureate in 2002. A fifth-generation Texan, Martha currently writes lyrics for composers Henry Flurry and George Chave. Her poems have appeared in *The Aurorean, Curbside Review, and* other print and web-based publications. (60)

Mary Margaret Carlisle, born in Dallas, is a Councilor for the Poetry Society of Texas and the founder and President of the Gulf Coast Poets. Project Director of *Sol Magazine,* she also chairs *Ampersand Poetry Journal's* Board of Directors. Founder of the Coffee Oasis Reading Series, Carlisle is a member of The Texas Association of Creative Writing Teachers, the Bay Area Writers League, and the Academy of American Poets, among others. (80)

Barbara Youngblood Carr has published thirteen books of poetry/prose and short stories based on her Cherokee heritage and her Texas/Southwestern/Southern upbringing. Host of Borders-on-the-Word poetry venue, she has served as a Board member of Austin International

Poetry Festival for sixteen years. She is also the editor for *A Galaxy of Verse,* DreamersThree Press and Little Chicken Fried Books. (74)

Mike Carter and his wife Salma spent three years as missionaries in China. Before passing away in 2005, he wrote four theology books, one novel, and numerous poems. (194)

Robin Cate lives and writes in the Rio Grande Valley, where she is a charter member of a writing group in Harlingen. She was featured at the first International Poetry Fest in the Valley. Author of a wide variety of publications, she is ever an observer. (195)

Dane Cervine's poems have appeared in various journals, including *The Hudson Review, The Sun,* and the *Atlanta Review.* Adrienne Rich chose Dane's poem "The Jeweled Net of Indra" as the winning entry in the 2005 National Writers Union competition. Dane's new book of the same title was published in 2007 by Plain View Press. He is a member of the Emerald Street Writers in Santa Cruz, California, where he serves as county Chief of Children's Mental Health. (141)

Lois V. Chapman, a member of the Poetry Society of Texas since 1984, is a retired ten-year Board member and recipient of two service awards— The President's Award and The Hilton Ross Greer Outstanding Service Award. Currently a Councilor-at-Large, Chapman has been published in several anthologies, including some of PST's annual awards books, as well as *Lucidity, Encore,* and *The Survivor.* (70)

Leah Chin Christian studied English and Spanish at the University of Texas before moving on to the University of Wisconsin to start an MA program in Comparative Literature. (103)

Robert Elzy Cogswell, an Austin poet retired from librarianship, edits the *Newsletter* of the Austin Poetry Society. In 2007, he was a Poet of the Week on the *Poetry Super Highway.* His poems have been published or are forthcoming in *Borderlands, The Texas Observer, farfelu, diverse-city, Muse & Stone, Green Hills Literary Lantern, Consciousness, Literature and the Arts, Passager, Lilliput Review,* and elsewhere. Earlier in life, he was a panhandler in Manhattan. (10)

SuzAnne C. Cole writes from a studio in the Texas Hill Country. She has published more than 350 poems, essays, short stories and articles in commercial and literary magazines, anthologies, and newspapers. She has been both a juried and featured poet at the Houston Poetry Fest, and she once won a haiku festival in Japan. Recently she received first prize in poetry from the Greater New Braunfels Arts Council. (52, 76, 79)

Nancy Kenney Connolly has authored three books—*The Color of Dust, 33 Shades of Green* (with artist Jeannine Sharkey), and *Second Wind*. She has won the Christina Sergeyevna Award at the Austin International Poetry Festival and the 2002 *Main Street Rag* Chapbook contest for *I Take This World*, poems of India. Nineteen of her poems appear in an anthology, *In These Latitudes*, published by Wings Press in 2008. She currently lives in Carrboro, North Carolina. (72, 132)

Sarah Cortez, author of *How to Undress a Cop* (Arte Público, 2000) is the winner of the 1999 PEN Texas Literary award in poetry. Cortez has edited *Urban-Speak: Poetry of the City* and *Windows into My World: Latino Youth Write Their Lives*, recently awarded the 2008 Skipping Stones Honor Award. A police officer since 1993, Cortez is currently focusing on a collection of non-fiction writing by law enforcement personnel about policing in America. (104)

Carol K. Cotten is a retired middle school, high school, and university English teacher whose poems have appeared in *Avocet: A Journal of Nature Poetry, TimeSlice, Edgar Literary Magazine, Bayou, English Journal, English in Texas, di-verse-city* and other publications. A juried poet at the 2004 Houston Poetry Fest and the Featured Poet for the 2006 Fest, Cotten is also the former editor of the quarterly journal *Spiky Palm*. (56, 67)

Carol Cullar, upon retirement from teaching art eight years ago, established the Rio Bravo Nature Center Foundation, of which she is President and Executive Director. Her publications include poems in the *Southern Humanities Review, The Wisconsin Review, Talus and Scree, The New York Quarterly*, and others, as well as her collection, *Pagan Heart*, and five chapbooks, including *Inexplicable Burnings*, winner of the Press of the Guadalupe's 1992 chapbook contest. (4, 66)

Carolyn A. Dahl's poems and essays have been published in *Camas, Sojourn, TimeSlice, Suddenly III and IV, Reading Lips, Women Artists' Datebook*, and *The Weight of Addition*. Dahl was a finalist in the PEN Texas nonfiction competition and has been awarded residencies to Hedgebrook Writers' Colony and the Vermont Studio Center. Also an artist, she is the author of two art books, *Natural Impressions* (Watson-Guptill) and *Transforming Fabric* (Krause). (42, 61, 168)

Betty Davis has published in over seventy literary journals and anthologies including *Poetry* and *Buffalo Spree*. At the University of Houston, she worked with a group to co-sponsor the UH Writer's Conferences. In 1999 Davis and Lianne Mercer launched the *Texas Poetry Calendar*, which they co-edited until it was turned over to Dos Gatos

Press. Now 82, she lives in a senior independent living center in Houston, the city she has called home for sixty years. (17, 114, 145)

Solana DeLámant is a PhD student of Humanities at the University of Texas at Dallas. DeLámant earned her BA in Anthropology and holds both an MFA in Modern Dance and an MFA in Creative Writing. *The Raintown Review* nominated her for a 2007 Pushcart. She has published in many national and international anthologies, and has three chapbooks as well. (166)

Jeffrey DeLotto, Professor of English in the School of Arts and Sciences at Texas Wesleyan University in Fort Worth, has published a chapbook entitled *Voices at the Door*, the Southwest Poets Series winner from the Maverick Press, and *Days of a Chameleon: Collected Poems*. He has been a Fulbright Lecturer in American Literature at the University of Plovdiv in Bulgaria, and he also serves as Poetry Editor for the international on-line journal *AmarilloBay.org* (81)

James O. Dobbs, born in the Panhandle in 1924, is a retired minister. He has been a member of state and national poetry societies and has been published in the Poetry Society of Texas *Yearbook*, as well as *Grist, Suddenly, Galaxy of Verse*, and several newspapers and journals. In 2004, he published, *Four Score*, a full-length collection of poems. In addition to writing poetry, he paints watercolors. (16, 38, 124)

Mary Margaret Dougherty's poetry is inspired by South Texas, the place and its people, where she has lived most of her life. Her poetry has appeared in *American Cowboy, Rope Burns*, and *English Journal*. She has been invited to read her poetry at the National Cowboy Symposium & Celebration, the Fulton Heritage Celebration, the Goliad Ranching Heritage Celebration, and the South Texas Ranching Heritage Festival. She lives in George West, Texas. (15)

Cyra S. Dumitru, born in Holland and raised in Connecticut and Ohio, has lived in San Antonio for nearly 28 years. She teaches writing and literature courses at St. Mary's University. The author of three books of poems, she is an avid, year-round swimmer. (62, 130, 153)

Doris Duncan taught English for 27 years, part of that time with a class of senior creative writers. Since her retirement in 1994, she has written short stories and poetry and joined the local chapter of the Texas Poetry Society. She has won Midland College's poetry contest and the Levitt Poetry contest. (182)

Peggy Lin Duthie, a Lubbock native, lives in Nashville, Tennessee. She is a Kentucky Colonel and a Unitarian Universalist lay preacher whose poems have appeared in *The Bedside Guide to No Tell Motel, Becoming Fire, Dwarf Stars, Rhymes for Adults, Ripple Effect,* and other anthologies, as well as in journals such as *Boxcar Poetry Review, Contemporary Rhyme, Dead Mule, the Fiddlehead, flashquake, Southern Gothic,* and *Strange Horizons.* (16, 122)

Mary C. Earle, a native San Antonian and an Episcopal priest, is the author of three books and co-author of two. Her poetry has appeared in *Windhover, Concho River Review, The Solitary Voice, New Texas, The San Antonio Express-News* and various anthologies. Her most recent work, *The Desert Mothers: Spiritual Practices from Women of the Wilderness* (Morehouse, 2007), is available as an audio CD. (59)

Lynn Edge divides her time between the Texas Coast and the Hill Country. Many of her haibun have appeared in online journals and recently in the print journals *Frogpond* and *Modern Haiku.* (184)

Chris Ellery is a professor of English at Angelo State University and the former poetry editor of *Concho River Review,* where he serves as book review editor. His poems have appeared in numerous journals, including *Rock & Sling, Cimarron Review, Tar River Review, New Texas,* and *descant.* His books include *Quarry,* a chapbook (Mountain Muse Press, 2004), and *All This Light We Live In,* his first full-length collection (Panther Creek Press, 2006). (150)

Susan J. Erickson, of Bellingham, Washington, has a poetry chapbook, *The Art of Departure* (Egress Studio Press, 2003). Her work has appeared in *Clackamas Literary Review, Switched-on Gutenberg, PoetryMagazine.com, Raven Chronicles, The Lyric* and various anthologies. She is an organizer of the Poet as Art reading series, which features outstanding poets from the Pacific Northwest. (89)

Carolyn Tourney Florek is a poet, visual artist, and publisher from Houston. Co-founder of Mutabilis Press, a non-profit literary press, she has been published in *Illya's Honey* and the Houston Poetry Fest anthology, with work forthcoming in the *Texas Review.* (128)

Lorena Flores-Knight is the Managing Editor of *Del Sol Review,* who otherwise spends her time working a "regular" job. She has three beautiful children and a husband who regularly keep her laughing. Her only wish is that she had more time to read and write. (129)

Peter Fogo is the author of two novels, *Nightsong* (1998) and *The Salvaged Wheel* (2006). (147)

Larry L. Fontenot has published in *Arrowsmith, Boxcar Poetry Review, Chachalaca Poetry Review, Curbside Review, Pebble Lake Review, Red River Review, RiverSedge,* and *Sulphur River Literary Review.* His chapbook, *Choices & Consequences,* was the winner of the Maverick Press 1996 Southwest Poets' Series Chapbook competition. Fontenot also won the 2000 *Alsop Review* Poetry Competition and the Dallas Poets Community's 2008 Annual Chapbook contest. (107)

Karen Gerhardt Fort, a sixth-generation Texan and a native of Waco, is the author of numerous books, articles, and poems. A graduate of Baylor University with an MA in Museum Studies, Fort is a museum consultant. She and her husband, author and museum consultant Thomas A. Fort, live in the Rio Grande Valley. (86)

Suzanne Freeman's poems have appeared in publications ranging from *Social Anarchism* to *The Journal of the American Medical Association.* Her novella, *Omnibo,* won the Clay Reynolds Novella Prize and was published in 2007 by Texas Review Press. She lives in Ingram, Texas.

Virginia Frey serves as a Councilor for the Poetry Society of Texas and as a poetry contest judge. She has authored seven books of special occasion poems. (18, 85, 123)

Geneva Fulgham is a retired teacher of English and journalism. She writes mysteries, essays, short stories, and poetry. A widow, she has two children, Mary and Joel, both professional musicians. (20, 74)

Shearle Furnish has taught at colleges and universities in Kentucky, North Carolina, and—for eighteen years—in Texas, where until 2007 he was Professor of English and department head at West Texas A&M University. Furnish is now Founding Dean of the College of Liberal Arts and Social Sciences at Youngstown State University, in Youngstown, Ohio. (54)

tony gallucci finished among the top independent poets at the 1998 National Slam Championship. He has been broadcast on *MTV, AustinUnScene,* and *channelAustin's EXSE Poetry Showcase.* His spoken word CD *Vignettes from the Edge of Humanity* is due for release in fall 2008. Also an actor and director, he is employed by the Hill Country Youth Ranch to work with abused and abandoned children in media, theatre, film, and music. (73)

John Gorman lives in Galveston and teaches literature and creative writing at the University of Houston-Clear Lake. His poem "Slice of Life" was chosen First Place in the 2009 Texas Poetry Calendar Awards by Benjamin Alire Sáenz. (186)

Lyman Grant currently serves as Dean of the Arts and Humanities Division at Austin Community College, sometimes teaching an introductory poetry writing workshop there. He has published dozens of poems, essays, and reviews—mostly in small, regional journals—and two volumes of poetry, *The Road Home* and *Text and Commentary*. In addition, he has published two textbooks and edited two books on regional literature. (186)

Abigail Green is a seventh-generation Texan, born in a September heat wave in Austin and raised in the shallow end of Barton Springs. National Science Fellow and winner of the Spring UT Writing Contest, her work is influenced by an intimate connection with the natural world. Green is working on her PhD at the California Institute of Technology, where she hopes to use insights from microbial ecology to help sustain and recover natural ecosystems. (88)

John Grey is an Australian-born poet, but a U.S. resident since the late seventies, who works as a financial systems analyst. He has recently been published in *Slant, Briar Cliff Review* and *Albatross*, with work forthcoming in *Poetry East, Cape Rock* and *RE:AL*. (128)

Nanette Guadiano-Campos is a writer and teacher whose poetry has appeared in numerous publications, including *Literary Mama, Borderlands*, and *Bordersenses*. Her personal essay, "Uprooted," is included in the anthology *Fifteen Candles: A Tale of Taffeta, Hairspray, Drunk Uncles, and Other Quinceañera Stories* (Harper Collins, 2007). She lives in San Antonio with her husband and two daughters. (41)

Laurie A. Guerrero's work has appeared or is forthcoming in *Palo Alto Review, Global City Review, Literary Mama, BorderSenses, Feminist Studies, Meridians*, and others. Her first book, *Babies Under the Skin*, won the Panhandler Publishing Chapbook Award. A graduate of Smith College and three-time winner of the Rosemary Thomas Poetry Prize, Guerrero has recently returned to San Antonio, where she was born and raised. (32, 170)

Laura Quinn Guidry's poetry has appeared in *The Texas Review, Concho River Review, Louisiana Literature*, and *Earth's Daughters*. Her poems have also been published in the anthologies *In the Eye* and *The Weight of Addition*; others are forthcoming in *In These Latitudes: Ten Contemporary Poets*. She lives in Houston and Carmine, Texas. (109)

Trudy S. Guinee, a graduate of Duke University and the Vermont College MFA in Writing program, lives in Houston. She is working on a manuscript combining her poems and her *plein-air* sketches from nature. (29, 69)

John G. Hammond is a poet, essayist, and book reviewer who lives with his wife Susan in The Woodlands, Texas. His poetry has appeared in numerous publications, including *Southern Poetry Review, The Texas Observer*, and the anthology *Between Heaven and Texas*. He has published book reviews in *The New Orleans Review, San Antonio Express-News*, and *Pif Magazine*. His article "Why Poetry Matters" was published in 2008 by Palabras Press. (23)

Shirley Jones Handley lives in Harlingen, Texas. She has numerous poems in anthologies and literary publications. She has published a children's book, *They Had a Dream, a History*, as well as a volume of poetry, *How Do You Measure a Hero* (Eakin Press). (147)

Jerri Buckingham Hardesty lives in the woods of Alabama with her husband, Kirk, and too many animals. Through their nonprofit organization, New Dawn Unlimited, they focus on poetry publishing, production, performance, promotion, preservation, and education. They also organize live poetry events. Hardesty has received dozens of awards and honors for both written and spoken word/performance poetry. (63)

Joyce Pounds Hardy, an alumnus of Rice University, won the Texas Writer's Recognition Award given by the Texas Commission on the Arts for her first book of poetry, *The Reluctant Hunter* (Latitudes Press, 1990). Other books include *French Windows* (Eakin Press), the memoir *Surviving Aunt Ruth*, and *Roads to Forgotten Texas* (Texas Review Press, 2004), a collection of black and white photographs by Tommy LaVergne with accompanying poems by Hardy. (161)

Penny Harter's most recent collection is *The Night Marsh* (WordTech Editions, 2008). Widely published, she has won three poetry fellowships from the New Jersey State Council on the Arts, as well as the Mary Carolyn Davies Award from the Poetry Society of America, and the William O. Douglas Nature Writing Award. Having moved back to New Jersey from Santa Fe in 2002, she is a teaching poet for the New Jersey State Council on the Arts. (123)

Michelle Hartman lives at the Fort Worth Home for the Terminally Bewildered and has had poems published in *Illya's Honey, Red River Review, Sojourn, descant*, and the anthology *The Weight of Addition*. She has a poem forthcoming in *Concho River Review*. (116)

Ralph Hausser, a graduate of California State University, Northridge, has had poems appear in *di-verse-city*, *farfelu*, *Pebble Lake Review*, *Poetography*, and numerous other journals and reviews. His poem "Passenger Station, Texas" took First Place in the 2006 Texas Poetry Calendar Awards. After many false starts, Hausser has branched into writing short speculative fiction and is currently working on his first novel, *Quarantine*. (144, 189)

Kurt Heinzelman is a Professor of English at the University of Texas at Austin, and Director of the Creative Writing Program. He has been the Pforzheimer Senior Fellow and Executive Curator at the Harry Ransom Humanities Research Center, a Fulbright Fellow, a Danforth Foundation Fellow, and a Fellow of the Society for the Humanities at Cornell University. Recently elected to the Texas Institute of Letters, Heinzelman has published two volumes of poetry *The Halfway Tree* and *Black Butterflies*, both finalists for the Natalie Ornish Prize. (159)

Margaret Ellis Hill, a keen observer of life and beauty, works to hone the craft of poetry by attending local critique workshops and advanced poetry sessions, including Centrum where she studied under Lynn Emanuel. Her work can be found in many magazines and anthologies, both on and off line. *Close Company*, her first poetry book, was published in 2003. (82, 178)

Michael Hill, who grew up in Wisconsin, holds a bachelor's degree in Music History from the University of North Texas and a Master of Library and Information Science from the University of Washington. After six years spent living in the Pacific Northwest, Michael and his family re-relocated to Austin in 2006. In addition to writing the occasional poem, Michael is a singer, songwriter and guitarist with three solo recordings to his credit. (106)

Shirley Hill is a poet who lives in Fort Worth. (112)

Bradley Earle Hoge lives in Spring, Texas, with his wife and three children. He teaches natural science at the University of Houston-Downtown. His most recent poems appear in *Tertulia*, *Chronogram*, *Elegant Thorn Review*, *LanguageandCulture*, *Concho River Review*, *Aurora Review*, and *Stickman Review*. (34, 118)

James Hoggard, named Poet Laureate of Texas for 2000, is an award-winning author of seventeen books, including novels, stories, collections of poems and translations. His most recent book, *Wearing the River: New Poems* (Wings Press) won the PEN Southwest Poetry Award for 2007. Former president of The Texas Institute of Letters, he has published in *Harvard Review*, *Southwest Review*, *Partisan Review*, *Manoa*, and many others. Seven

of his plays have been produced, including two in New York. (179)

J. Paul Holcomb, a past president and long-time officer of the Poetry Society of Texas, writes a column, "Discussing Poetic Forms with the Poet from Double Oak," for the *DFW Poetry Review*. His first book of poems, *Love, or Something Like It*, won the Lucidity Chapbook Award (Bear House Publishing, 1997). His second, *Looking for Love in the Telecom Corridor*, won the Eakin Memorial Book Award from Eakin Press in 2004. (78, 111)

Janis Butler Holm, a native Houstonian, lives in Athens, Ohio, where she has served as Associate Editor for the film journal *Wide Angle*. Her essays, stories, poems, and performance pieces have appeared in small press, national, and international magazines. *Jonesing for Samantha*, a one-act play, was produced at Manhattan Theatre Source last fall. (105)

G. A. Hottel, of Santa Rosa, California, is a retired high school teacher who lived as a child on a small farm near Arlington, Texas. The farm is now a parking lot for Six Flags Over Texas. (28)

Ann Howells is a longtime member of the Dallas Poets Community and has been managing editor of its semi-annual journal, *Illya's Honey*, for ten years. In 2001, she was named a "distinguished poet of Dallas" by the Dallas Public Library. In 2005, her poem "La Resistancia" was nominated for a Pushcart Prize. In 2007, her chapbook, *Black Crow in Flight*, was published by Main Street Rag. She has had work appear most recently in *Avocet* and *Plainsongs*. (26, 127)

Albert Huffstickler, "the Bard of Hyde Park," passed away in 2002, but not before publishing hundreds of poems and more than thirty collections, including Austin Book Award winners *Walking Wounded* (1989) and *Working On My Death Chant* (1991). (125)

Cindy Huyser is a poet, computer programmer, and former power plant operator. A native of Detroit, she has lived in Austin, for most of her adult life. Her work has appeared in a variety of publications, including *The Comstock Review*, *Borderlands: Texas Poetry Review*, *Wild Plum*, each *di-verse-city* anthology from Austin International Poetry Festival, and *Layers* (Plain View Press, 1994). Cindy co-edited the 2009 *Texas Poetry Calendar* with Scott Wiggerman. (91)

Judy Jensen's poems have appeared in journals and anthologies such as *The Prose Poem: An International Journal* and *Letters to the World: Poems from the Wom-Po Listserv*. Two poems are on display with the Blanton Museum's Poetry Project. She won First Place in the 2008 Texas

Poetry Calendar Awards and has been nominated for a Pushcart Prize. Float Press, which she co-founded, produces letter-pressed broadsides with work by major American poets. (10)

Maggie Jochild, who has twice won the Astraea Lesbian Writers award for her poetry, is currently working on a trilogy of novels. She's been an activist in most social change movements in this country and has raised a daughter with another woman. She is a staff writer for Group News Blog and maintains her own literary blog, Meta Watershed. (40, 58, 185)

Charlotte Jones, after a twenty year career as a computer scientist and management consultant, promised herself she would do something more creative with her life and began writing and taking pictures. Her work has appeared in over seventy literary and commercial magazines. Her first play was produced in 2003 in Texas and played in New York in 2004. She is at work on her first novel, about a teen accused of arson. (92, 148)

Marcelle H. Kasprowicz was born in France and lives in Austin, Texas. She writes in English and French. In 2001, her poem "House of Bones" won first prize in the Austin International Poetry Festival awards. Her poems have appeared in several magazines, anthologies, and online. Her first book of poems, *Organza Skies*, was published in 2005. (65, 126)

Claire Keyes, who lives in Marblehead, Massachusetts, is attached to Texas through family members who live in Central Texas. She is the author of *The Aesthetics of Power: The Poetry of Adrienne Rich*. Her poems and reviews have appeared in *Calyx, Blueline,* and *Valparaiso Review,* among others. Her chapbook, *Rising and Falling,* won the Foothills Poetry Competition, and a collection of poems, *The Question of Rapture,* was published by Mayapple Press in 2008. (112)

George Klawitter teaches literature at St. Edward's University in Austin. His poems have appeared in *The James White Review, Poetry Northwest, Poet Lore, Evergreen Chronicles, Milkweed,* and *Cumberland Poetry Review.* His book *Let Orpheus Take Your Hand* won the Gival Press Poetry Award in 2002. His latest book of poetry, *The Agony of Words,* appeared in 2004. In 2007 he published *Holy Cross in Algeria,* a translation of 100 missionary letters. (117)

Quraysh Ali Lansana, Director of the Gwendolyn Brooks Center for Black Literature and Creative Writing at Chicago State University, is the author of *They Shall Run: Harriet Tubman Poems* (Third World Press, 2004); the poetry collection *Southside Rain* (Third World Press, 2000); *The Big World,* a children's book (Addison-Wesley, 1999);

and two poetry chapbooks. He is the editor of Glencoe/McGraw-Hill's *African American Literature Reader* and a former editor for *Black Issues Book Review.* (19)

Jim LaVilla-Havelin has appeared in the *Texas Poetry Calendar,* 2006 through 2009. His poem "World Trade" has been reprinted by Poetry in Motion for showing on Dallas buses. LaVilla-Havelin was the co-coordinator of San Antonio's 2008 Poetry Month events and calendar. He lives in Lytle, Texas, with his wife, Lucia LaVilla-Havelin, a fiber artist. (56, 92, 96)

Erica Lehrer is a poet, journalist and founding member of Net Poets Society, a Houston-based poets' group. Her writing has appeared in both national and regional publications. She is a graduate of Princeton University and the NYU School of Law. (20)

Lynn Lewis used to tell people that she wrote out of self-defense, as a matter of survival, that if she didn't write, she would explode. Her roots are intensely rural and southern, and she apologizes for neither. She grew up on her family's hundred-year-old homestead in Cass County, Texas. She has been most influenced by Lucille Clifton, Billy Collins, and Toni Morrison. (187)

Perie Longo, the current Poet Laureate of Santa Barbara, California, has published three books of poetry—*Milking the Earth, The Privacy of Wind,* and *With Nothing Behind But Sky: A Journey through Grief* (Artamo Press, 2006). For over twenty years she has led poetry workshops for the annual Santa Barbara Writers Conference. Her work has appeared in *Atlanta Review, Connecticut Review, Flyway, International Poetry Review, Nimrod,* and many other journals. (194)

Peggy Zuleika Lynch, nominated seven times for a Pushcart, is a poet and lecturer in her native state of Texas. The Paris American Academy in Paris, France named her Poet Laureate and permanent Poet-in-Residence. In 1983 she and her husband co-founded Poetry in the Arts to promote poetry, music, and art. In 2005 at the 18th World Congress of Poets, she was crowned Poet Laureate International and became the permanent Vice-President of the United Poets Laureate International. (38, 146)

Shellie Lyon, of Camp Creek Lake, Texas, is currently working on a collection of poems and photographs. (9, 181)

Budd Powell Mahan has served as the President of both the Poetry Society of Texas and the National Federation of State Poetry Societies. He won the Eakin Manuscript Competition in 2005, with *Falling to Earth,* and the Stevens Manuscript

Competition in 2006, with *Harvest*. After a fulfilling career as a public school teacher, he retired in 2002. (149)

Jean Donaldson Mahavier, of both Decatur, Georgia and San Leon, Texas, does volunteer teaching during the academic year in Georgia, giving classes in writing poetry, and spends summers at her home on Galveston Bay. She is currently writing a poetry exercise book for elementary students to aid them in critiquing their own work. (142)

Jean H. Marvin and husband Conrad have recently moved to Plano to be closer to family. She continues to focus her writing on children's fiction and poetry. (14, 24, 45, 115)

Janet McCann, published widely, has been teaching at Texas A&M since 1969. She received a National Endowment for the Arts award in 1989. Her most recent collection is *Emily's Dress* (Pecan Grove Press, 2004). (60)

Anne McCrady is a writer, speaker and social activist whose poetry and prose appear widely in journals, inspirational collections, and American and international anthologies. Her first poetry collection, *Along Greathouse Road*, won the 2003 Eakin Manuscript Award. Her poetry chapbook, *Under a Blameless Moon*, won the 2007 Pudding House Chapbook Competition. McCrady is the founder of *InSpiritry—Putting Words to Work for the Greater Good*. (5, 30, 64, 134, 158)

Chris McMillon is originally from Caddo Mills, Texas. After graduating from Texas A&M-Commerce, he taught English in Spain for nine years. He now lives in Belfast, Northern Ireland, and is married to an Irish girl. He takes American high school groups on a Harry Potter tour around England and Scotland every year. He has two Spanish cats that don't speak English. (162)

David Meischen, a native of rural South Texas, has work in *Two Southwests*, an anthology of poems from the Southwest of China and the United States (Virtual Artists Collective, 2008). His poetry has appeared in *Cider Press Review*, *The Southern Review*, *Southern Poetry Review*, *Borderlands*, and *Texas Poetry Journal*, among others. A fiction writer in the MFA program at Texas State University-San Marcos, Meischen is the co-founder of Dos Gatos Press, publisher of the *Texas Poetry Calendar*. (122, 154, 167)

Lianne Elizabeth Mercer edited and published the *Texas Poetry Calendar* from 1999 to 2005 with Betty Davis. She is a nurse, writer, and certified poetry therapist. Her work has been published in *American Journal of Nursing* and *What Wildness Is This: Women Write About the Southwest*. Her

short story, *"For Sale,"* was nominated for a Pushcart Prize in 2001. A memoir about her mother's last years, *Compassionate Witness: Before We Say Goodbye*, was published in 2005. (76, 166)

Ron Mohring's first book, *Survivable World*, won the 2003 Washington Prize. He lives in central Pennsylvania, teaches at Lycoming College, and runs Seven Kitchens, a micropress publishing poetry and fiction chapbooks. He maintains a blog at http://suppleamounts.blogspot.com. **(90)**

Karen Cecile Moon is a San Antonio-based poet. (178)

Katrinka Moore's chapbook, *This Is Not a Story* (Finishing Line Press, 2003) won the New Women's Voices Prize in Poetry. Moore's manuscript *Thief* was recently chosen as a finalist by the Cleveland State University Poetry Center's First Book competition and the Stan and Tom Wick Poetry Prize competition. Her poems have appeared in numerous magazines and anthologies, including *Georgetown Review* and *Stories from Where We Live: the Gulf Coast*. (148)

Sheila Tingley Moore is the president of the Alamo Area Poets of Texas and past president of the San Antonio Poets Association, where she has been the Poet Laureate for two years and Poet Emeritus for one year. She is also twice the winner of the Kitchener Foundation's Texas Senior Poet Laureate, and the vice-president of the San Antonio Poetry Fair. A former professor and teacher of high school English, she has published six volumes of poetry. (25, 49)

karla k. morton is author of the book/CD *Wee Cowrin' Timorous Beastie*, a unique blend of poetry, story and original Celtic music. She is a board member of both the Greater Denton Arts Council, and the Denton Poet's Assembly. She has been published in *Write Around the Corner*, *AmarilloBay*, *Concho River Review*, and the *Wichita Falls Literary and Art Review*, with work forthcoming in *descant* , *Southwestern American Literature*, *ARDENT*, and *Illya's Honey*. (99)

Sheryl L. Nelms has had over 4,500 poems, stories and articles published in everything from *Reader's Digest* and *Modern Maturity* to *Cricket* and *Kaleidoscope*. Essay editor of *Pen Woman*, the magazine of the National League of American Pen Women, and member of the Society of Southwestern Authors and the Abilene Writer's Guild, Nelms has thirteen collections of published poetry. (70)

Violette Newton of Beaumont, Texas, has published over twenty books, both poetry and fiction. She is a former Poet Laureate of Texas, Councilor at Large for The Poetry Society of Texas, and

Member of the Southeast Texas Women's Hall of Fame. Published in numerous anthologies and magazines, she is now 96 and still writes columns for the *Beaumont Enterprise*. (72, 175)

Yvonne Nunn was born on a ranch in Dunn, Texas, where she presently lives with her husband of 55 years, a retired Methodist minister. She started writing poetry in 1990 and was named the 2006 Texas Senior Poet Laureate by the Kitchener Foundation, a non-profit literary society in Springfield, Missouri, where she currently serves as Dean of Online Education. Nunn is the founder of the writing group Bards of a Feather, with members from around the world. (113)

Naomi Shihab Nye lives with her husband, photographer Michael Nye, in old downtown San Antonio, a block from the river. Nye is the author and/or editor of more than twenty volumes of poetry and fiction—many for young people—including the recent *Honeybee* (Greenwillow, 2008); *I'll Ask You Three Times, Are You Okay?*, which won the Friends of the Austin Public Library Texas Institute of Letters Award for 2007; and *You & Yours* (BOA Editions), which won the Isabella Gardner Poetry Prize. (161)

Katherine Durham Oldmixon, current president of the Austin Poetry Society, teaches writing and literature at Huston-Tillotson University. Her poems and photographs have appeared in print and online magazines, including *Borderlands*, *Utter, qarrtsiluni, Ellipsis, RE:AL, Passager*, and *Fieralingue Poet's Corner*. Oldmixon's chapbook *Water Signs*, a finalist for the New Women's Voices Chapbook Award, is forthcoming from Finishing Line Press. She is currently completing an MFA in Creative Writing from the University of New Orleans. (55)

Katie O'Sullivan always enjoyed writing but never became serious until her seven children were raised and her husband retired from their life abroad. After she settled in Houston, her original plan was a family memoir, but poetry keeps intruding. Her poems, essays and even a play have appeared in magazines ,journals, anthologies and on-line publications. (7)

Claire Ottenstein-Ross is the author of fourteen poetry books including children's, inspirational, and secular. She also edited the Poetry Society of Texas' *Book of the Year* for two years. President/Editor of Counterpoint Publishing Co., she has published poetry books for authors all over the U.S., including three Poets Laureate of Texas. Co-founder of Poets Northwest and Christian Writers Northwest, she has also been an editor for Christian Writers, Inc. (180)

Keddy Ann Outlaw is a Houston writer and artist disguised as a librarian. Her work has appeared in *Borderlands: Texas Poetry Review, Lilliput Review*, various *Papier Mâché* anthologies, *Texas Short Stories* and *Texas Short Stories 2*. She also enjoys the immediacy of writing as the "Lone Star Librarian" from her *Speed of Light* blog. (44)

Katie Oxford, born and raised in Beaumont, lives in Houston. Her first essay, "The Witch Within," was published in *The Houston Chronicle*. She was a juried poet in the Houston Poetry Festival in 2003 and 2007. Her poems have been published in the *Texas Poetry Calendar* and the *Bayou Review*. She is presently working on a memoir, *Broken Bowls and Wooden Spoons*. (68, 177)

Joy Palmer, a widely published author and speaker on leadership and organizations in both the U.K. and U.S., also writes poetry. She divides her time between Austin, New York and Washington, D.C. She co-produced a poetry/photography exhibit with New Zealand photographer Linda Young in 2008, and she is involved with *Diverse Youth*, an anthology produced each year as part of the Austin International Poetry Festival. (52, 132)

Mary G. Parham holds a PhD in Romance Linguistics and Literature from UCLA and writes in both English and Spanish. Awarded two Fulbright Scholar Grants, she is the co-author of *If Di Pin Neva Ben: Folklore and Legends of Belize*. Her poems have appeared in *Ventana Abierta, The Caribbean Writer, Atlanta Review* and other literary publications, as well as in several anthologies, including *The Weight of Addition*. (21, 120)

Leslie Patterson's stories and essays have appeared in *Fourth Genre, Bellevue Literary Review, Ballyhoo Stories, Matter*, and the 2007 Fish Publishing Prize Anthology. In 2006, she was the first prize winner of the Tiny Lights Publishing Essay Contest, and in 2008 she was the second prize winner of the Tallgrass Writers Competition. Currently at work on a historical novel, she lives in Fort Collins, Colorado. (36)

Michelle Paulsen is an Associate Professor of English at The Victoria College, where she teaches composition, literature, and creative writing and sponsors the VC Writer's Club. Widely published, she has three books of poetry and a Pushcart Prize nomination. (121)

Jackie Pelham of Conroe has published novels, short stories, poetry, and journalism. As publisher/editor of Stone River Press, she has published *Suddenly*, an anthology of Texas poets, and books by many Texas authors. (158)

Karen Peterson has had work appear in *Poetry, Quarterly West* and *American Fiction*, among others. Her itinerant musician father-in-law told her about the diner that appears in her poem "How They Ate in El Paso, 1932." She lives in Oak Park, Illinois. (11)

Aliene Pylant works at Richland Community College as a Senior Rehabilitation Specialist. Her poetry has appeared in *The Formalist, Raintown Review, Relief* and *Daughters of Sarah*. (18, 30)

Carolyn Luke Reding grew up on the Texas coast and lives in Austin. Her third collection of poetry, *Two Rivers Poetry: Interactive Poetry from the Brazos and the Colorado*, was published in 2007 by Poetry in the Arts, and includes her Pushcart-nominated poem, "Diffusion." Reding is the first-vice president and program chair of the Austin Poetry Society. She is currently seeking an MAR from the Episcopal Theological Seminary of the Southwest. (136)

Carol Coffee Reposa's poems and essays have appeared in *The Atlanta Review, The Formalist, The Texas Observer, Concho River Review, Passages North*, and other journals. Author of three books of poetry, Reposa has received three Pushcart Prize nominations and three Fulbright-Hays Fellowships for study abroad. When she is not teaching, she joyfully pursues three hobbies: jogging, singing, and spending time with her three grandchildren. (88, 102, 144, 156, 170)

Carol J. Rhodes, President of her own company, C R Business Services, conducts business communication workshops for the University of Houston's Small Business Development Center. Included among her writing credits are *The Houston Chronicle, Christian Science Monitor, Country Home, Texas, RE:AL*, and *Chicken Soup for the Girlfriend's* Soul. One of her plays was also showcased in a summer festival production of an off-Broadway theatre. (34, 143)

John E. Rice is a writer and artist living and working in Houston but born in Galveston, who still crosses the causeway onto The Island with some regularity. His published works have appeared in *Texas Magazine* and *Sol Magazine*, and the anthologies *TimeSlice* and *The Weight of Addition*. His art is in several private collections around the world. A 45-year veteran of the International Maritime Industry, he is president of Resk Maritime Resources, Inc. (124, 137, 155)

Sally Wells Ridgway's poetry has been published in literary journals such as *Gulf Coast, Sulphur River Literary Review*, and *Nimrod*. She has led creative writing workshops, taught English at high schools in Galveston and Houston, and has an MFA in Writing from Vermont College. (13)

Lee Robinson practiced law for over twenty years in Charleston, South Carolina, where she was elected the first female president of the bar association. *Hearsay* (Fordham University Press, 2004), her first collection of poetry, won the 2004 Poets Out Loud Prize and the Writers' League of Texas Violet Crown Award for best book of poetry. Robinson has published in such publications as *Harper's, Crab Orchard Review, Southern Poetry Review*, and *Texas Observer*. (32, 163)

Margie McCreless Roe, retired from teaching college English at San Antonio College, now spends time in Estes Park, Colorado, and with grandchildren in Austin. Roe has published in *Concho River Review, Texas Observer, Christian Science Monitor, Christian Century*, and *Borderlands*, among others. Her credits include two volumes of poetry, *Flight Patterns* (River Lily Press), and *Call and Response*, forthcoming from Pecan Grove Press. (133, 172)

Del Marie Rogers' most recent book, *She'll Never Want More than This* (Firewheel Press, 2002), was a finalist for the Texas Institute of Letters' Best Book of Poetry. Her work has appeared in a number of magazines and Texas anthologies, including *Roundup* (Prickly Pear Press, 1997); *Is This Forever, Or What?* (Greenwillow Books, 2004); and *In These Latitudes* (Wings Press, 2008). (193)

Deborah Rossel teaches college composition in Connecticut. With an MFA in creative writing from Lesley University, she was awarded the Leslie Leeds Poetry Prize in 2002 and the Leo Connellan Poetry Prize in 2003. She is the assistant editor of *Tuesday; An Art Project*. (142)

Kay Gorges Schill grew up in Harlingen, lived in Houston for fifty years, and now resides in Kerrville, Texas. Her work has appeared in the *Houston Chronicle* and the *Hill Country Mountain Sun*. She has also written the history of a Houston law firm. (24)

Anne Schneider, a writer and visual artist, leads mask workshops across Texas and in 2005 opened Ventana al Cielo Studio in Kerrville, where she leads creative arts workshops, hosts guest artists' workshops, and has taught Tai Chi and reiki classes. Her book *Breath Found along the Way* is an artistic blend of poetry and images of her face-cast mask art. She also designed and wrote the *Reiki Card Deck: 50 Guided Energy Techniques* (Fair Winds Press). (6, 43, 95)

Steven Schroeder is the co-founder of the Virtual Artists Collective, which has published seventeen full length collections of poetry and five chapbooks since it began in 2004. He teaches at the University of Chicago and at Shenzhen University in China. He has published two chapbooks, *Theory of Cats* and *Revolutionary Patience*, and two full-length collections, *Fallen Prose* and *The Imperfection of the Eye*. *Six Stops South* is forthcoming from Cherry Grove Collections in March 2009. (39)

Jan Seale, a native Texan, lives in McAllen in the Lower Rio Grande Valley. Among her poetry books are *Bonds* and *Sharing the House* (RiverSedge Press); *The Yin of It* (Pecan Grove Press); and *The Wonder Is: New and Selected Poems 1974-2004* (Panther Creek Press). A member of the Texas Institute of Letters, she has published in *The Texas Monthly*, *The Yale Review*, and *The Chicago Tribune*, among others. A collection of short stories, *Airlift*, was published by TCU Press. (50, 71, 94, 105)

Joan Seifert, of San Antonio, is a native Texan who loves writing about the Southwest. She has published in *Concho River Review*, *St. Anthony Messenger*, *Westward Quarterly*, *New Texas*, and various anthologies. She has edited the poetry section of the *San Antonio Express-News*, and has produced chapbooks read throughout San Antonio. (146)

Naomi Stroud Simmons is the author of eight chapbooks including, *I Will Miss You Gently*, which has been used in grief therapy groups. Her work appears in *Encore*, *Suddenly*, *Lucidity*, *Mooncrossed*, *New Texas*, *Windhover*, *Grasslands*, *Aries* and numerous other journals. She has also appeared in the anthologies *I Feel a Little Jumpy Around You* and *Is This Forever or What?*—both edited by Naomi Shihab Nye. (171)

Sheryl Slocum, raised in Colorado and Wyoming, now lives in Wisconsin, where she teaches English as a second language. Her poetry has appeared in the *Wisconsin Poets' Calendar* and the *Anglican Theological Review*. Slocum's poem, "Fly Fishing," won first place in the 2005 John Lehman Poetry contest for the Wisconsin Academy of Sciences, Arts and Letters and was published in the *Wisconsin Academy Review*. (8)

Betsy Slyker, a transplanted Midwestener, has lived in Texas for over fifty years. She has published in numerous anthologies and plans to keep writing as long as she can. (51)

John E. Smelcer is the author of over thirty books, including his Pulitzer-Prize-nominated collections *Songs from an Outcast* and *Without Reservations*. For fifteen years he has been poetry editor at *Rosebud* magazine. He is currently the Clifford D. Clark Fellow of English and Creative Writing at Binghamton University. (118)

Glen Sorestad, a Canadian poet, is a frequent visitor to Texas. The author of eighteen books of poetry, he was the first Poet Laureate of Saskatchewan and is a Life Member of the League of Canadian Poets. His poetry has been published in literary publications in many countries and translated into a half-dozen languages. Sorestad's latest poetry books include *Leaving Holds Me Here: Selected Poems 1975-2000* and *Blood & Bone, Ice & Stone* (2005). (119)

Sharman Speed (Houston, Texas) is an artist and poet. Her poetry ranges from ekphrastic to spiritual to whimsical. (102)

Marilyn Stacy, a Professor Emeritus, is a psychotherapist in private practice in Dallas. She served as president of the Poetry Society of Texas, 2006-2008. Her publications include articles, short fiction, and numerous poems, including two books, *Along the Path* and *Dreams and Other Altered States of Consciousness*. (44)

Cathy Stern received the PEN Southwest Houston Discovery Prize for Poetry in 1985. Her work has appeared in *The Paris Review*, *The New Republic*, and *Shenandoah*; poems and an interview appeared in the anthology *A Wider Giving: Women Writing After a Long Silence*. She has taught English and Creative Writing at the University of Houston-Downtown, poetry workshops for Inprint, and is now teaching memoir classes for seniors, also through Inprint. (174)

Dr. Charles A. Stone is a native of Green Bay, Wisconsin and has doctoral degrees from Marquette University and Johns Hopkins University. His poetry has appeared in various medical journals, online, and in several poetry journals and anthologies, including *Wild Plum* and *di-verse-city*. (173)

Jack Swanzy is a poet based in Fredericksburg, Texas. (139)

Marilynn Talal won a National Endowment for the Arts Creative Writing Fellowship and the Stella Erhardt Memorial Fellowship of the University of Houston, where she earned a PhD in Creative Writing. She also won a Fellowship in Literature from the Writers' League of Texas. She has published more than a hundred poems in venues such as *Poetry*, *The Paris Review*, *The New Republic*, *Southern Poetry Review*, and *The Louisville Journal*. (28)

Chuck Taylor has a book of poems forthcoming, *Li Po Laughing at the Lonely Moon*, from Pecan Grove Press. He has written two novels, *Drifter's Story*, and *Fogg in High School*. He has a collection of short stories about Austin, *The Lights of the City*. When rent and traffic got overwhelming, Taylor left Austin for College Station, where he teaches creative writing, American nature writing, and Beat literature at Texas A&M University. (110, 138)

Mary-Agnes Taylor, Distinguished Emerita Professor of English from Texas State University-San Marcos and Life Member of the Austin Poetry Society, began writing poetry after she retired from the classroom in 1995. Her poems in *Big Land, Big Sky, Big Hair,* dedicated to the memory of Captain George P. Taylor, USNR, 1915-1984, are from the unpublished collection *Conversations with George.* She and George met as college freshmen, married, and spent some twenty years as a Navy family. (3, 14, 26, 36, 84)

Sandra Gail Teichmann was born and grew up in Salida, Colorado. She received her MFA in Writing from Vermont College, and her PhD in English from Florida State University. She teaches literature and writing at West Texas A&M University and lives and writes in Canyon, Texas. She is the author of *Slow Mud* (Pecan Grove Press). (131)

Susan Terris' poetry books include *Contrariwise* (Time Being Books, 2008), *Natural Defenses* (Marsh Hawk Press), *Fire Is Favorable to the Dreamer* (Arctos Press), and *Poetic License* (Adastra Press). A poem from *Field* was published in *Pushcart Prize XXXI,* and work also appears in *The Iowa Review, Beloit Poetry Review, Calyx, Colorado Review, Prairie Schooner,* and *Ploughshares.* For seven years she was editor of *Runes,* and now she, with Ilya Kaminsky, is poetry editor of *In Posse Review.* (66)

Larry D. Thomas was appointed by the Texas Legislature as the 2008 Texas Poet Laureate. He has published nine collections of poems, most recently, *Larry D. Thomas: New and Selected Poems,* issued by TCU Press as the fourth volume of the Texas Poets Laureate Series. Among the prizes and awards he has received are the 2004 Violet Crown Award, the 2003 Western Heritage Award, two *Texas Review* Poetry Prizes, and two Pushcart Prize nominations. (63)

David J. Thompson grew up in Hyde Park, New York, but had the pleasure of living in Bryan, Texas, from 1982 to 1986 and Denton, Texas, from 1991 to 1997. He now lives and teaches English in the Detroit area. (37)

Mel C. Thompson, raised in North Orange County, California, migrated to the San Francisco Bay Area in 1989, where he formed Cyborg Productions, a well-known underground press in the early 1990s, which published such artistic luminaries as Michael McClure. Thompson's civil rights work for free speech and his legal work for California workers resulted in worldwide publicity in such outlets as *USA Today* and NPR. He was later a radio personality at KMEL. (135)

Mary Tindall, of Whitehouse, Texas, is a haiku writer, sunflower gardener, and bird watcher. She thinks of writing haiku as putting a puzzle together. She writes stories and verse for her family. Pastimes include browsing antiques in Texas towns and tea partying with grandchildren. She is listed in *Who's Who Among American Teachers.* She lives with Lynn, her husband of forty years, in her house of 36 years. (78, 87)

Rawdon Tomlinson teaches creative writing, most recently at the University of Colorado at Denver. His newest book is *Geromimo After Kaski-yeh* (LSU Press, 2007). (79)

Rebecca Hatcher Travis is an enrolled citizen of the Chickasaw Nation with deep roots in both Texas and Indian Territory, Oklahoma. She is a member of Wordcraft Circle of Native Writers and Storytellers, Bay Area Writers League, and Gulf Coast Poets. Her first poetry collection, *Picked Apart the Bones,* won the 2006 First Book Award for Poetry from the Native Writers' Circle of the Americas; it is scheduled for publication in the fall of 2008. (157)

Meredith Trede, one of the founding publishers of Toadlily Press, has published in *Blue Mesa Review, Gargoyle, Heliotrope, The Paris Review, Runes, 13th Moon,* and *West Branch.* Her chapbook, *Out of the Book,* was in *Desire Path,* the inaugural volume of The Quartet Series. She has an MFA from Sarah Lawrence College and has held residency fellowships at Ragdale, Saltonstall, and the Virginia Center for the Creative Arts. (33)

Pamela Uschuk is the author of four books of poems, *Finding Peaches in the Desert, One-Legged Dancer, Scattered Risks* (nominated for a Pulitzer Prize), and *Without the Comfort of Stars: New and Selected Poems* (Sampark Press, 2007). Editor-in-chief of *Cutthroat: A Journal of the Arts,* Uschuk is a professor of Creative Writing and Director of the Southwest Writers Institute at Fort Lewis College in Durango, Colorado. A new collection of poems, *Crazy Love,* is due out in 2009 from Wings Press. (160)

Ryan G. Van Cleave's most recent books include a poetry collection, *The Magical Breasts of Britney Spears* (Red Hen Press, 2006), and a creative writing textbook, *Behind the Short Story: From First to Final Draft* (Allyn & Bacon/ Longman, 2006). He is the Creative Director of New Realm Productions and Director of C&R Press, a nonprofit poetry press. (6)

Dia VanGunten is a surrealist and writer from Austin, Texas. She is an ink-smudged paper airplane with crooked wings. She's interested in exploring the realm of magical-realism in a modern urban context. "Landscaping" was written during a month-long obsession with the haiku form, during which countless haikus came from everyday ingredients such as fried eggs or bathtubs. (80)

Beverly Voss, a psychotherapist and Interplay teacher, also gardens, paints, dances, and teaches creative journaling workshops. Her recent poetry has been published in the books *What the Body Wants* and *Walking in Two Worlds*. (180)

Jane Butkin Wagner's poetry, fiction, and essays have appeared in over a hundred publications, including *Pearl*, *Rattle*, *Mothers and Daughters*, *Essential Love*, *Nerve Cowboy*, *Owen Wister Review*, *Red Wheelbarrow*, *The Jewish Women's Literary Annual*, *Redoubt*, and *Suddenly*. She edited the anthology *We Used To Be Wives: Divorce Unveiled Through Poetry* (Fithian Press, 2002). (35)

Loretta Diane Walker has recently completed 25 years of teaching music to elementary children in Odessa, Texas. She has remained active in her community through membership in organizations such as Delta Sigma Theta Sorority, the Odessa Cultural Council, and the Permian Basin Poetry Society. Her poetry has appeared in *Harp-String Poetry Journal* and the Poetry Society of Texas *Book of the Year 2008*. Her own book, *Word Flirtations*, is available in trade paperback. (174)

Ken Wheatcroft-Pardue has been lucky enough to call Fort Worth, Texas, home for a dozen years. He is an English-as-a-Second Language teacher at an inner-city high school. Most recently he has had poems in *Illya's Honey*, *miller's pond*, *Wavelength*, *Borderlands*, and the now defunct on-line journal *redriverreview.com*. He has poems forthcoming in *The Texas Observer*. (40, 62, 116)

Gerald R. Wheeler's photography, fiction and poetry have appeared in numerous literary reviews and national magazines, including *North American Review*, *Louisiana Literature*, *Iron Horse Literary Review*, *Antietam Review*, *Kaleidoscope*, *RiversEdge*, *Big Muddy*, *Equine Journal*, *Horse Illustration*, and *Antique Power*. (51)

Lounell Whitaker, a member of the Beaumont Poetry Society, has published in several literary publications, including *Suddenly*, *Lucidity*, and yearbooks of the Poetry Society of Texas. She has published a book of her family's history, *Echoes*. She is also the winner of the 2008 Eakin Manuscript Publication Prize for a children's book. (77, 81, 190)

Anthony Russell White, a native Texan, has been living in Northern California since 1954. Previously an art historian specializing in 20th-century American printmakers, he returned to poetry after an epiphany in a field of yellow tulips in La Conner, Washington, in 1992. He has published over 200 poems and eight chapbooks. A full-length collection, *The Faith of Leaping*, will be published by Spire Press later this year. (27, 53, 100, 111)

Scott Wiggerman is the author of *Vegetables and Other Relationships* and editor of the *Texas Poetry Calendar*. His work has appeared in journals such as *Borderlands*, *Poesia*, *Contemporary Sonnet*, *Visions International*, *Spillway*, *Sojourn*, and the *Paterson Literary Review*, as well as books such as *The Weight of Addition* and *Poem, Revised*. He has spent much of 2008 preparing and editing *Big Land, Big Sky, Big Hair: Best of the Texas Poetry Calendar*. (58, 83, 162, 190)

Steve Wilson, whose books include *Allegory Dance* and *The Singapore Express*, has poems out or forthcoming in *Beloit Poetry Journal*, *Commonweal*, *North American Review*, *America*, *The Christian Science Monitor*, *Blue Unicorn*, *New Orleans Review*, *The Christian Century*, *New American Writing*, and other journals. He is also represented in anthologies such as *Stories from Where We Live: The Gulf Coast* (Milkweed Editions) and *American Diaspora: Poetry of Displacement* (University of Iowa). (154, 169, 183)

Junette Kirkham Woller, a long-time resident of San Antonio, has a background in the Fine and Performing Arts and Journalism. Her work has appeared in books such as *Chocolate for a Teen's Soul*, *Quotable Texas Women*, and *Summer Shorts*. She has work forthcoming in *Memory Bridge* and *Sweet Dreams*. Her experience as a music teacher, professional model, handspinner, weaver, calligrapher, bookbinder, and toastmaster are resources for her work. (117)

Robert Wynne earned his MFA in Creative Writing from Antioch University. He is the author of six chapbooks and two full-length books of poetry, *Remembering How to Sleep*, the recipient of the 2006 Eakin Book Award, and *Museum of Parallel Art*, published in 2008 by Tebot Bach Press. He has won numerous prizes, and his poetry has appeared in magazines and anthologies throughout North America. He, his wife, and his daughter live in Burleson, Texas. (155)

Acknowledgments

All poems in *Big Land, Big Sky, Big Hair* were published in *Texas Poetry Calendar*, 1999-2008. In addition, Dos Gatos Press acknowledges the following:

Valerie Martin Bailey, "Lullaby for a Tiny Texas Town," in *Inkwell Echoes* (San Antonio Poets Association, 1985-86) and in *Voices Along the River* (San Antonio Poetry Fair, 2001).

Rebecca Balcárcel, "Crepe Myrtles" in *South Dakota Review*, 38, No.2 (2000).

Linda Banks, "East of Amarillo" in *Book of the Year* (Poetry Society of Texas, 2003) and in *Poetic Drawls* (Deep Creek Hills Press, 2003).

Bruce Bond, "Feast of the Seven Sorrows" in *Western Humanities Review* and in *Radiography* (BOA Editions, 1997).

Lana Book, "My Next 50" in *Coming Full Circle* (Plain View Press, 1996).

Nancy Kenney Connolly "At the Pedernales River Gorge" in *Texas Observer*, 18 July 2002.

Carol Cullar, "Rising Star, Texas, 1898/1992" in *Southwestern American Literature*, 18, No. 2 (1992) and in *This Hunger* (Maverick Press, 1993); "Totem to a Dying Breed" in *Borderlands*, 5 (1994). Both poems in *Texas in Poetry: A 150 Year Anthology* (Center for Texas Studies, 1994).

Betty Davis, "I Am Lucy" in *Clark Street* (1998).

Chris Ellery, "Lift-off from DFW Just after Dark" in *Quarry* (Mountain Muse Press, 2004).

Larry Fontenot "Wile E. Coyote's Lament" in *Conspire*, 1998, and in *The Year's Best Fantasy and Horror, 12th Ed.* (St. Martin's Press, 1999).

Karen Gerhardt Fort, "Alluvial Deposit" in the *San Antonio Express-News*, 28 November 2004.

Virginia Frey, "They Follow Dreams" in *Book of the Year* (Poetry Society of Texas, 2000) and in *The Robert Frost Festival of Poetry Anthology* (Summer, 2001).

Joyce Pounds Hardy, "Island Ladies" in *Roads to Forgotten Texas* (Texas Review Press, 2004).

Penny Harter, "Driving West Texas" in *Lizard Light: Poems from the Earth* (Sherman Asher, 1998).

James Hoggard, "May" in *Wearing The River: New Poems* (Wings Press, 2005).

Marcelle H. Kasprowicz, "Field Hospital" in *Organza Skies* (De Lodis, 2005).

Budd Powell Mahan, "What Land?" in *Book of the Year* (Poetry Society of Texas, 1999).

Anne McCrady, "Opening Day" in *Along Greathouse Road* (Eakin Press, 2004).

Katrinka Moore, "Reading a Map" in *This Is Not a Story* (Finishing Line Press, 2003).

Naomi Shihab Nye, "Click" in *Honeybee* (Greenwillow Books, 2008).

Sheryl L. Nelms, "Heirloom Hocked" in *For She Is The Tree of Life: Grandmothers Through The Eyes of Women Writers* (Conari Press, 1996).

Claire Ottenstein-Ross, "The 'Fraidy Hole" in *Book of the Year* (Poetry Society of Texas, 1997) and in *Suddenly III* (Martin House, 2000).

Jackie Pelham, "Blue Norther" in *Writer's Lifeline*, October 1990.

Jan Seale, "A Collared Peccary by Any Other Name" in *Mesquite Review*, Feb/Mar 2000; "Javelinas" as the frontispiece in *Javelinas* (Texas Tech Univ. Press, 2006); "Airborne Fantasy" and "Mockingbird (Mimus Polyglottos)" (titled "Au Contraire") in *Valley Ark* (Knowing Press, 2005).

Mary-Agnes Taylor, "Liberation" in *di-verse-city* (2002); "Time Exposure" in *di-verse-city* (2004).

Larry Thomas, "The Mare" in *Stark Beauty* (Timberline Press, 2005).

Mary Tindall, "blazing fields flicker" and "mockingbird's music" in *Behind the Picket Fence* (Rose Garden Poetry Society, 2007).

Rawdon Tomlinson, "Deep Red" in *Deep Red* (Univ. of Florida Press, 1995).

Jane Butkin Wagner, "Honk If You're My Daddy" in *Buffalo Bones* (1998) and in *Unlikely Stories* (1999).

Scott Wiggerman, "Wilshire Woods" in *Limestone Circle*, 3, 1999, and in *Vegetables and Other Relationships* (Plain View Press, 2000); "The Pecan Trees" in *Other Voices Poetry Project*, 12, 2005.

Steve Wilson, "Clear Night, After a September Storm" in *The Christian Century*, 12-19 September 2001.

Junette Kirkham Woller, "Visit to the Texas State Aquarium" (titled "Traditional Haiku: A Visit to the Texas State Aquarium") in *Texas Maritime Literature Awards* (U.S. Maritime Literature Awards, 1998).